Better Homes and Gardens®

Christmas
from the Heart™

All Through the House

BETTER HOMES AND GARDENS® BOOKS
Des Moines, Iowa

BETTER HOMES AND GARDENS® BOOKS
An Imprint of Meredith® Books

CHRISTMAS FROM THE HEART
Editor: Carol Field Dahlstrom
Contributing Graphic Designer: Gayle Schadendorf
Technical Editor: Colleen Johnson
Administrative Assistant: Peggy Daugherty
Contributing Technical Illustrator: Chris Neubauer Graphics
Production Manager: Douglas Johnston

Editor-in-Chief, Book Group: James D. Blume
Director, New Product Development: Ray Wolf
Managing Editor: Christopher Cavanaugh

Meredith Publishing Group
President, Publishing Group: Christopher Little
Vice President and Publishing Director: John P. Loughlin

Meredith Corporation
Chairman of the Board and Chief Executive Officer: Jack D. Rehm
President and Chief Operating Officer: William T. Kerr

Chairman of the Executive Committee: E.T. Meredith III

All of us at Better Homes and Gardens® Books are dedicated to providing you with the information and ideas you need to create beautiful and useful projects. We guarantee your satisfaction with this book for as long as you own it. We welcome your questions, comments, or suggestions. Please write to us at: Better Homes and Gardens® Books, RW 235, 1716 Locust Street, Des Moines, IA 50309-3023.

If you would like to order additional copies of any of our books, call 1-800-678-2803 or check with your local bookstore.

Cover: Photograph by Hopkins Associates

 Our "Mark of Excellence" craft seal assures you that every project in this publication has been constructed and checked under the direction of the crafts experts at Better Homes and Gardens® Cross Stitch & Country Crafts® magazine.

 Our seal assures you that every recipe in *Christmas from the Heart* has been tested in the Better Homes and Gardens® Test Kitchen. This means that each recipe is practical and reliable, and meets our high standards of taste appeal. We guarantee your satisfaction with this book for as long as you own it.

ISSN: 1081-4698
ISBN: 0-696-20447-9 (hardcover)
ISBN: 0-696-20559-9 (softcover)

Peek through the door of a house filled with the holiday spirit and you can see the excitement. The magic of the season has spread to all parts of the house—from the elegant handcrafted ornaments on the tree, to sweet homemade goodies in the kitchen. Children are whispering secret wishes to Grandpa, and Mother is staying up late to finish that very special handmade gift. The family is together again, with just a bit more laughter, a few more hugs, and a little more kindness in the air.
It is Christmastime.

We wish you the merriest of holidays and that this book will bring joy and happiness to your heart and home as you experience Christmas

All Through the House

Contents

Heartwarming Welcomes

When friends and family come to your home to share the warmth of the holiday season, greet them with open arms and a house filled with handcrafted treasures and home-baked delights.

Elegant Holiday Wreath	8	Christening Dress	10–11
Peacock Appliqué Vest	9	Appetizer Medley	12–13
Welcome Sampler	10		

A Storybook Christmas

Treat your family to the magic of a child's Christmas with this fun- and fantasy-filled collection. Each toy, trim, and tasty bite takes its inspiration from the tales and poems of childhood.

Alice-in-Wonderland Fantasy	20–21	Baskets of Goodies	28–29
Alice-in-Wonderland Ornaments	22	Red Riding Hood Cape	30
Christmas Tea Cozy	23	Red Riding Hood Topsy-Turvy Doll	31
Christmas Tea Party	24–25	Three Christmas Pies	32–33
Teatime Quilt	26	Soft-as-Kittens Mittens	34
Teacup Gifts	27	Gingerbread Boy Sweater	35

Best-Selling Bazaar

The trick to a successful bazaar is filling it with quick-to-make (and quick-to-sell) crafts and foods. To get you off to a good start, here are a dozen sure-fire ideas.

Chocolate Brownie Mix	58	Raggedy Snowman	60
Gumdrop Cookie Mix	58	Elf and Reindeer Party Favors	60
Chocolate Cashew Clusters	59	Faux Cookie Ornaments	60
Applesauce-Rhubarb Muffins	59	Fun Felt Santa Claus	61
Peppery-Plum Barbeque Sauce	59	Snowman Button Covers and	
Whole Wheat Pretzels	59	Lapel Pin	61

In a Twinkling

Put sparkle on the season with clever touches of lighting—inside and out. Choose from center-pieces and mantel displays to "icicles" on the roof and luminaries that brighten the way home.

Lavender Centerpiece	70	Beaded Icicles	72
Sparkling Holly Garland	70	Country Luminaries	73
Glittering Goblets	71	Glimmering Icicles	74
Twinkling Jar	71	Happy, Lighted Snowman	75

Christmas Past

Join us for a look into the history and the delights of a Victorian Christmas, then re-create these period ornaments and recipes for your own 19th-century Victorian-inspired holiday.

Victorian Elegance	80–81	Scallop Oval with Sunburst	89
The Tree of Christmas Past	82	Angel on Crepe Paper Circle	91
Satin Ribbon Stocking	85	Tinsel Heart	91
Gingerbread Noah's Ark	86	Victorian Star Tree Topper	93
Sweet Treats	87	Trumpeting Cherub on Circle	93
Victorian Steamed Pudding	88	Diamond Tinsel Ornament	94
Beaded Star Ornament	89		

Family Celebrations

It's easy to turn a family meal into a celebration. Just sprinkle the menu with a few new recipes and add table decorations. You'll love our brunch, light supper, and snack-time ideas.

Strawberry French Toast	102–103	Apricot Bavarian Crème with	
Orange-Spinach Toss	102–103	Raspberry Sauce	106–107
Candy-Stripes Place Settings	104	Christmas Bell Bread	106–107
Candy-Cane Cake	105	Oyster Stew with Vegetables	106–107
		Crocheted Christmas Bells	106–107

A Collector's Dream

If you're a doll fancier or you know a collector, you'll love this playtime place, where moppets, cherubs, snowmen, and Santas of all sorts pop up, thanks to your sewing and crafting skills.

Sweet Angel Baby	116	Herbal Snowman	119
Treetop Angel	117	Primitive Santa	120
Frosty, No-Sew Snow Family	118	Lovable Elf Santa	121

The Giving Tree

The Christmas tree stands at the heart of all holiday decorating, imparting the spirit of this most giving season. In its honor, we offer glorious ornamentals and gift-wraps to make yours extra special.

Quilted Christmas-Wreath		Sugar-Sweet Garland Treat	142
Tree Skirt and Wall Hanging	140	Bookmark Trio	143
Jack-in-the-Box Ornament	140	Ribbon Bow	143
Roly-Poly Santa	141	Tasseled Snow Lace	143
The Christmas Rose	141	Gilded Christmas Corsage	144
Good-Dog Treat	141	Holiday Dress-Up	144
Embroidered Doily Ornament	141	Kid's Crayon Rain-"Bow"	144
Tatted Jingle Flake	142	Fun-Burst Fantasy	145
Crystal-Clear Hobby Ornaments	142	Beaded, Bejeweled, and Bedazzling	145

Heartwarming Welcomes

As friends and family come to share the warmth of the holiday season, greet them with open arms to a home filled with handcrafted treasures and home-baked treats. From a glorious fruit-and-dried-florals wreath to appetizers as festive and good to eat as they are easy to make, all of these items create special season's greetings. Touched by your heart, right from the start, your guests will know they're welcome to your joyous and fun-filled home.

PHOTOGRAPHER: HOPKINS ASSOCIATES

Elegant Holiday Wreath

Greet holiday visitors at the door with this regally adorned Christmas wreath. Created using a pineapple, purple grape clusters made from tiny Christmas balls, and satin ribbons, the wreath will say "Merry Christmas" during the holiday season. Instructions for the wreath and the tiny grape clusters are on page 14.

DESIGNER: GERRI BAUMAN ● PHOTOGRAPHER: HOPKINS ASSOCIATES

Peacock Appliqué Vest

What fun to strut your holiday stuff wearing this proud-as-a-peacock appliqué. Applied to a purchased vest or one made from a commercial pattern, the individual fabric pieces are machine-appliquéd using variegated metallic thread. Add elegant embellishments with charms, faceted beads, seed beads, and shiny rayon-floss embroidery. Instructions and the full-size pattern are on pages 14–16.

DESIGNER: MARGARET SINDELAR ● PHOTOGRAPHER: HOPKINS ASSOCIATES

Welcome Sampler

*Show off your talents at Christmastime by displaying
your needlework for all to enjoy. Our Welcome Sampler
can be quickly cross-stitched on 16-count Aida and
embellished with gold blending filament and beads.
Instructions and chart are on page 16.*

DESIGNER: PATRICIA ANDRLE ● PHOTOGRAPHER: HOPKINS ASSOCIATES

Christening Dress

*Grandma will love giving the newest family member
this christening dress. Knit in softest Luster Sheen
yarn, it has a ribbed yoke and sleeves, shoulder picots,
back-button closure, and scalloped collar that repeats
the lacy body pattern. Instructions begin on page 16.*

DESIGNER: ANN SMITH ● PHOTOGRAPHER: HOPKINS ASSOCIATES

Appetizer Medley

*Every guest, young and old, will love
our appetizer sampler plate filled with goodies
to try. The variety of colors and textures of
the hors d'oeuvres makes a beautiful
Christmas platter. Recipes begin on page 17.*

PHOTOGRAPHER: HOPKINS ASSOCIATES

ELEGANT HOLIDAY WREATH

As shown on page 8.

MATERIALS

26-inch-diameter evergreen wreath

Hot-glue gun; glue sticks

3 yards 1-inch-wide burgundy reversible-stripe satin ribbon

7 yards 2-inch-wide periwinkle satin-center organdy ribbon

24 peacock feathers

17 dried red roses

14 pieces of dried purple stock

12 pieces of dried white statice

Four pieces of reindeer moss

Four 4-inch-long pinecones

Nine lemon leaves

White spray paint

Gold metallic paint

One pineapple; knife

Liquid floor wax; floral picks

For grape clusters

½- to ¾-inch-diameter glass Christmas balls on wires

Purple flat spray paint

Small silk leaves

Floral wire

Green floral tape

INSTRUCTIONS

Slice a ¾-inch-thick section from one side of the pineapple. Dip both sections into floor wax to seal; let dry. Position large pineapple section at the bottom of the wreath slightly left of center. Secure with picks. Fasten remaining section to the top right of wreath in the same manner.

Make an 11-loop bow from periwinkle ribbon. Secure center of the bow with floral wire. Wire the bow to the bottom center of the wreath.

For each grape cluster, paint balls purple; let dry. Tape two balls together with floral tape. Tape balls to cluster, one at a time, until nine are joined. Add silk leaves. Poke wire end of cluster into wreath.

Arrange burgundy ribbon on wreath as desired. Hot-glue the remaining materials to the wreath, beginning with the roses, stock, statice, reindeer moss, and pinecones. Space each type of material evenly around the wreath for a well balanced arrangement.

Spray-paint lemon leaves white; let dry. Accent edges and veins of the leaves with gold metallic paint; let dry. Glue peacock feathers and lemon leaves onto the wreath.

PEACOCK VEST

As shown on page 9, appliqué measures 8x13¾ inches.

MATERIALS

Lined vest pattern in desired size

Rose washed-silk and dark gold lining fabrics in amounts specified on pattern envelope

Medium-weight fusible interfacing in same amount required for rose washed-silk fabric

Tracing paper

10x20-inch piece of paper-backed iron-on adhesive

6x18-inch piece of iridescent gold taffeta

PEACOCK APPLIQUÉ VEST

SATIN STITCH

╱ Beak

STEM STITCH

╱ Beak

╱ Eye

╱ Branches

BEADS

• Eye

● Head

● Leaves

LEAVES

✕ Leaves

Satin Stitch

Stem Stitch

- **4x8-inch piece each of green silk, iridescent navy taffeta, and purple taffeta**
- **4x6-inch piece of iridescent violet silk**
- **2x3-inch piece of purple silk**
- **8x16-inch piece of tear-away fabric stabilizer**
- **Dark gold thread**
- **Metallic purple-and-green variegated machine appliqué thread**
- **Lavender, gold, and dark aqua rayon embroidery floss**
- **Embroidery needle**
- **½x¾-inch plastic sew-on leaf charms: four silver, three dark green, and three light green**
- **Four 4-millimeter crystal green faceted beads**
- **Six 2x6-millimeter crystal pink flower-shaped beads**
- **Four green seed beads**
- **Six pink seed beads**
- **One black seed bead**

INSTRUCTIONS

Cut out vest pieces from the silk, lining, and interfacing, according to pattern instructions. Fuse interfacing to wrong side of silk pieces. Sew vest front pieces together.

Trace pieces (A, B, C) of one feather and each peacock section (A, B, D, E, F), *opposite,* onto the tracing paper. Cut out.

Draw around pattern pieces, right side down, on paper side of iron-on adhesive. Trace pieces for 10 feathers. Cut out adhesive pieces, leaving extra adhesive around smaller pieces. Following manufacturer's instructions, fuse A pieces to wrong side of iridescent gold taffeta, B pieces to green silk, C pieces to purple taffeta, D piece to iridescent violet silk, E pieces to iridescent navy taffeta, and F piece to purple silk. Cut out all pieces.

Remove paper from the iron-on adhesive. Layer and arrange pieces on right vest front, placing peacock head 2½ inches below shoulder seam. Fuse, using a press cloth.

Baste tear-away stabilizer to the underside of the vest front beneath

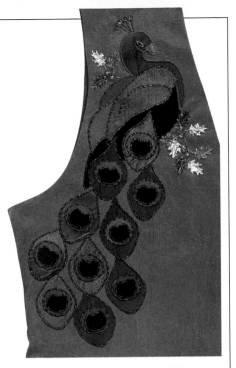

the peacock. Using dark gold thread, machine-satin-stitch around peacock's head and neck section. Using metallic thread, machine-satin-stitch around all other pieces, along head feather lines, and along dotted center line of wing.

Use two plies lavender rayon floss to stem-stitch around eye. Use two plies gold rayon floss to satin-stitch

PEACOCK VEST

beak, then stem-stitch around beak. Use three plies dark aqua rayon floss to stem-stitch branches.

Finish sewing vest according to pattern instructions. Use one ply aqua rayon floss to sew leaves to ends of branches. With thread, sew green faceted bead anchored with a green seed bead to end of each head feather. Sew pink flower bead anchored with a pink seed bead to each dot among the branches. Sew black seed bead to eye.

WELCOME SAMPLER

As shown on page 10.

MATERIALS

FABRIC
9x12-inch piece of 16-count white Aida cloth

THREADS
Cotton embroidery floss in colors listed in key

Blending filament in color listed in key

SUPPLIES
Needle; embroidery hoop

Seed beads in color listed in key

Desired frame and mat

INSTRUCTIONS

Zigzag edges of Aida cloth to prevent fraying. Find center of chart, *below,* and center of fabric; begin stitching there. Use two plies of floss for cross-stitches. Work the blended needle as specified in key. Attach beads with old gold (DMC 677) floss. Press stitchery; frame.

CHRISTENING DRESS

As shown on page 11. Directions are for infants size 6 to 9 months. Finished chest size = 19 inches. Skill Level: Intermediate.

MATERIALS

SUPPLIES
J. & P. Coats Luster Sheen Article A95 (1.75-ounce or 50-gram ball): six balls of white (001)

Size 5 circular knitting needle, 24-inch length

Size 4 circular knitting needle, 16-inch length

Tapestry needle

Two stitch markers

Nine ¼-inch heart buttons

GAUGE:
In Body Pat St with larger circular needle, 7 sts = 1 inch. In ribbing with larger circular needle, 8 sts = 1 inch.

BODY PATTERN STITCH

Row 1: (rs): K 1, * yo, (k 1, p 1) 7 times, k 1, yo, k 1; rep from * across.

Row 2: K 1, * p 2, (k 1, p 1) 7 times, p 1, k 1; rep from * across.

WELCOME SAMPLER		
ANCHOR		DMC
860	☒	522 Dark olive drab
859	⊟	523 Medium olive drab
102	◯	550 Violet
861	▲	935 Pine green
1028	⊞	3685 Mauve
BLENDED NEEDLE		
886	·	677 Old gold (1X) and 002 Kreinik gold blending filament (1X)
888	✳	3045 Dark yellow beige (1X) and 002 Kreinik gold blending filament (1X)
887	▽	3046 Medium yellow beige (1X) and 002 Kreinik gold blending filament (1X)
BEADS		
	◯	00557 Gold Mill Hill seed bead

Stitch count: 60 high x 104 wide

Finished design sizes:
16-count fabric – 3¾ x 6½ inches
14-count fabric – 4¼ x 7⅜ inches
18-count fabric – 3⅓ x 5¾ inches

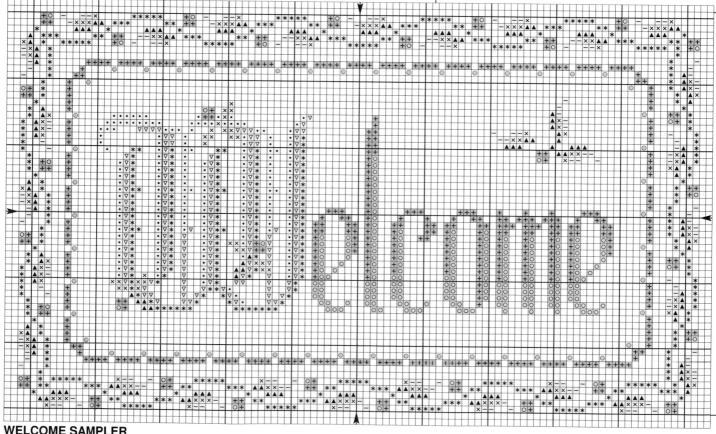

WELCOME SAMPLER

Row 3: K 2, * yo, (k 1, p 1) 7 times, k 1, yo, k 3; rep from * across, ending last rep k 2.

Row 4: K 2, * p 2, (k 1, p 1) 7 times, p 1, k 3; rep from * across, ending last rep k 2.

Row 5: K 3, * yo, (k 1, p 1) 7 times, k 1, yo, k 5; rep from * across, ending last rep k 3.

Row 6: K 3, * p 2, (k 1, p 1) 7 times, p 1, k 5; rep from * across, ending last rep k 3.

Row 7: K 4, * yo, (k 1, p 1) 7 times, k 1, yo, k 7; rep from * across, ending last rep k 4.

Row 8: K 4, * p 2, (k 1, p 1) 7 times, p 1, k 7, rep from *, end last rep k 4.

Row 9: K 5, * (ssk) 3 times, sl 1 st knitwise, k 2 tog, psso, (k 2 tog) 3 times, k 9; rep from * across, ending last rep k 5.

Row 10: Purl.

INSTRUCTIONS

Work back and forth using a circular needle, rather than in rounds, for the entire garment.

For skirt, with larger needle, cast on 241 sts. Work Body Pat to about 16½ inches from beg, ending with Row 9. To shape waist, p 28, * p 2 tog; rep from * across to last 29 sts, p 29 = 149 sts.

For bodice, Ribbing Row 1 (rs): K 1, * p 1, k 1; rep from * across.

Ribbing Row 2: P 1, * k 1, p 1; rep from * across. Work even in ribbing to ½ inch from first Row 1.

For armholes, rib 36 sts; join new ball and rib 77 sts; join a new ball and rib to end. Working 3 pieces at the same time and with separate balls, cont est rib pat to 2½ inches from first Row 1 for front and to 4 inches for backs.

For backs, after pieces measure 4 inches from first Row 1, bind off all sts.

For front, when piece is 2½ inches from first Row 1, shape neck as follows: rib 28 sts, join new strand and bind off the center 21 sts, rib to end. Work sides separately and at the same time, bind off at each neck edge every other row as follows: 4 sts once, 3 sts once, 2 sts once, and

1 st once = 18 sts rem for each shoulder. Work even to same length as backs. Bind off all sts.

For sleeves (make 2), with larger needle, cast on 59 sts. Work ribbing as for Bodice for 4 rows. Dec 1 st each edge every fourth row 7 times, cont in est rib pat. When piece is 4½ inches from beg, end with Row 2. K 1, * k 2 tog; rep from * across = 23 sts. K 2 rows for garter- st border. P 1 row. For eyelets, k 1, * yo, k 2 tog; rep from * across. Beg with a p row, work 3 rows st st. Bind off all sts. Fold eyelet row in half to ws; hem. Sew sleeve seam.

For collar, with larger needle, cast on 97 sts. Work rows 1—10 of Body Pat. K 10, * k 2 tog; rep from * across to last 10 sts, k 10 = 59 sts. P 1 row. Bind off all sts.

Sew shoulder seams. With rs facing and smaller needle, pick up and k 59 sts around neck. K 6 rows for garter st. Bind off all sts loosely and knitwise. With rs of each piece facing, sew bound-off edge of collar to first garter-st row.

For back plackets, sew skirt to 3 inches from bodice. With rs facing and smaller needle, begin at right back edge to pick up and k 52 sts, place a marker, pick up and k 1 sts at seam, place marker, pick up and k 52 sts along left back edge.

Row 1: K to 2 sts before first marker, k 2 tog, sl marker, k 1, sl marker, k 2 tog, k to end.

Row 2: K 2, * yo, k 2 tog, k 6; rep from * across for 5 buttonholes, yo, k 2 tog, k 5, k 2 tog, sl marker, k 2, sl marker, k 2 tog, k to end. Rep Row 1 twice more. Bind off all sts, knitwise.

For shoulder picots, place marker 2 inches from shoulder seam on front and back of bodice. With rs facing and larger needle, pick up and k 33 sts bet markers. Work 3 rows st st, beg with a p row. Work eyelets as for Sleeves. Work 3 rows st st, beg with a p row. Bind off all sts. Fold along eyelet row; hem.

Set in sleeves. Sew buttons opposite buttonholes. Sew 3 buttons to collar at center front, overlapping buttons. Weave in loose ends.

POLYNESIAN MEATBALLS
Pictured on page 13.

INGREDIENTS
- 1   beaten egg
- ¼   cup fine dry bread crumbs
- 2   tablespoons snipped fresh cilantro or parsley
- 2   cloves garlic, minced
- ⅛   teaspoon ground red pepper
- 1   pound lean ground beef
- ¼   cup finely chopped peanuts
- 1   20-ounce can pineapple chunks (juice pack), drained
- 1   8-ounce jar maraschino cherries
    Sweet-Sour Sauce

METHOD
Combine egg, bread crumbs, cilantro, garlic, ¼ teaspoon *salt,* and red pepper in a medium mixing bowl. Add beef and peanuts; mix well. Shape into 1-inch meatballs. Place in a 15x10x1-inch shallow baking pan. Bake in a 350° oven for 20 minutes or till no longer pink. Remove from oven. Drain. (To make ahead, cool meatballs, cover, and chill for up to 48 hours.)

Thread a pineapple chunk or cherry and a meatball on wooden toothpick. Return to baking pan. Repeat with the remaining fruit and the meatballs. Brush with Sweet-Sour Sauce.

Bake 5 to 8 minutes more or till heated through. (For chilled meatballs, bake 10 minutes.) In a small saucepan, heat remaining sauce till bubbly. Brush meatballs and fruit with sauce before serving. Makes 36 appetizers.

Sweet-Sour Sauce: In a small saucepan stir together ½ cup packed *brown sugar* and 4 teaspoons *cornstarch.* Stir in ½ cup *chicken broth;* ⅓ cup *red wine vinegar;* 2 tablespoons *corn syrup;* 2 tablespoons *soy sauce;* 1 clove *garlic,* minced; and 2 teaspoons grated *gingerroot.* Cook and stir till thickened and bubbly. Cook 2 minutes more. Use immediately. Or, cover and chill for up to 1 week. Makes about 1¼ cups.

MINI-CALZONES

Pictured on page 13.

INGREDIENTS

⅓ cup finely chopped pepperoni
¼ cup finely chopped green pepper
¼ cup pizza sauce
2 tablespoons finely chopped onion
½ teaspoon dried Italian seasoning, crushed
1 10-ounce package refrigerated pizza dough
1 beaten egg
Parmesan cheese (optional)

METHOD

Stir together pepperoni, green onion, pizza sauce, onion, and Italian seasoning in a small bowl.

Unroll dough. On lightly floured surface, roll dough into a 15-inch square. Cut into twenty-five 3-inch squares. Spoon a slightly rounded teaspoon of pepperoni mixture atop each square. Brush edges of each square with water. Lift one corner of each square and stretch dough over the filling to opposite corner, making a triangle. Press edges together; seal well with fingers or a fork. Arrange calzones on a greased baking sheet. Prick tops with a fork. Mix egg and 2 teaspoons *water;* brush over calzones.

Bake in a 425° oven for 10 to 12 minutes or till golden. During last 3 minutes of baking time, sprinkle with Parmesan cheese, if desired. Let stand 5 minutes before serving. Makes 25 appetizers.

NEW POTATO SKINS

Pictured on page 12.

INGREDIENTS

1 pound whole tiny new potatoes (10 to 12)
2 tablespoons nonfat plain yogurt
3 tablespoons light sour cream
2 tablespoons thinly sliced green onion
Freshly ground black pepper

METHOD

Scrub potatoes with a vegetable brush. Use a fork to prick the skins. Arrange potatoes on a microwave-safe plate. Micro-cook, uncovered, on high power for 7 to 9 minutes or till potatoes test done with a fork, turning potatoes over and rearranging halfway through the cooking time. Remove from oven and cool till potatoes are easy to handle.

Cut potatoes in half and place, cut side up, on same microwave-safe plate. With a small melon-ball scoop, remove some of the insides from each potato to make room for filling. Reserve centers for another use. (If desired, cover potatoes and refrigerate for up to 24 hours.)

To reheat, on a microwave-safe plate micro-cook potatoes, covered with vented plastic wrap, for 2 to 3 minutes or till heated through. Meanwhile, in a small bowl combine yogurt and sour cream. Place *2 teaspoons* of the mixture in *each* potato. Sprinkle *each* potato with green onion and pepper. Makes 20 to 24 servings.

EGGNOG

Pictured on page 12.

INGREDIENTS

6 beaten egg yolks
2¼ to 2½ cups milk
⅓ cup sugar
1 teaspoon vanilla
1 cup whipping cream
2 tablespoons sugar
Ground nutmeg

METHOD

Combine egg yolks, milk, and the ⅓ cup sugar in a large, heavy saucepan. Cook and stir over medium heat until mixture coats a metal spoon. Remove from heat.

Cool quickly by placing pan in a sink or bowl of ice water and stirring for 1 to 2 minutes.

Stir in the vanilla; chill for 4 to 24 hours.

At serving time, in a bowl whip the cream and the 2 tablespoons sugar till soft peaks form. Transfer chilled egg mixture to a punch bowl. Fold in whipped cream mixture. Serve at once. Sprinkle each serving with ground nutmeg. Makes about 10 (4-ounce) servings.

SPINACH DIP IN FRENCH BREAD

Pictured on page 12.

INGREDIENTS

2 10-ounce packages of frozen chopped spinach, thawed and well drained
1 8-ounce package light cream cheese (Neufchâtel), cut up
2 tablespoons milk
2 cloves garlic, minced
¼ teaspoon finely shredded lemon peel
1 tablespoon fresh lemon juice
2 teaspoons Worcestershire sauce
¼ teaspoon salt
¼ teaspoon bottled hot pepper sauce
¼ cup sliced green onion
1 16-ounce round loaf French bread (about 6 inches in diameter)
Assorted vegetables

METHOD

For dip, in a large mixer bowl combine the drained spinach, cream cheese, milk, minced garlic, shredded lemon peel, lemon juice, Worcestershire sauce, salt, and hot pepper sauce. Beat with an electric mixer on medium speed until combined. Stir in the sliced onion. Cover and chill until serving time.

For bread bowl, slice 1 inch off top of French bread loaf and reserve. With a large spoon, scoop out the inside of the bread loaf, leaving about a ½-inch-thick shell. Reserve insides for another use or cut bread pieces into cubes to use as dippers.

Spoon the spinach mixture into the hollowed bread shell. Serve loaf surrounded by vegetables. Makes 24 appetizer servings.

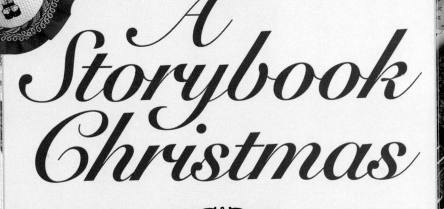

A Storybook Christmas

---

*Recreate the magic of a child's Christmas
with our collection of ideas for the holidays inspired
by charming tales from yesteryear. From knitted
mittens and magical dolls to holiday pies and baskets
for Grandma, our collection of festive ideas helps
make this the perfect Storybook Christmas.*

PHOTOGRAPHER: HOPKINS ASSOCIATES

Alice-in-Wonderland Fantasy

Christmas is coming! Hurry, don't be late. Start preparing now for this most important date. Small trims take on larger-than-life appeal gathered on this Alice-in-Wonderland delight. At the heart of the theme are the cross-stitched character trims. Painted tea sets, a playing-card garland, and golden watches add more holiday sparkle. Instructions begin on page 36.

TREE STYLING: CAROL DAHLSTROM, MARGARET SINDELAR, DONNA CHESNUT
PHOTOGRAPHER: HOPKINS ASSOCIATES

Alice-in-Wonderland Ornaments

*These Christmas branches read like the pages from a storybook.
Colorful, whimsical, and straight from Alice's curious dream, comes this
delightful cross-stitch collection. Make Alice and her friends—the White
Rabbit, Queen of Hearts, Mad Hatter, Cheshire Cat, and Tweedledum
and Tweedledee. Instructions and charts are on pages 36–39.*

DESIGNER: LINDA GORDANIER JARY ● PHOTOGRAPHER: HOPKINS ASSOCIATES

Christmas Tea Cozy

Welcome your guests to a spot of spiced tea and a setting so enchanting, they'll want to linger for a holiday chat. The centerpiece is a ribbon embroidered teapot cozy, done in seven quick stitches. Instructions begin on page 39.

DESIGNER: MARGARET SINDELAR ● PHOTOGRAPHER: HOPKINS ASSOCIATES

Christmas Tea Party

In Wonderland, the table is always set for teatime. Here, it's readied as an extra-festive occasion for invited Christmas guests. The spread offers an assortment of scrumptious appetizers from purchased petit fours to orange scones and finger sandwiches that you can prepare in the wink of an eye. Recipes begin on page 41.

PHOTOGRAPHER: HOPKINS ASSOCIATES

Teatime Quilt

Here's a sweet quilt that'll suit you to a "tea." A petite 16x19 inches, it's set with six tiny cups, each flavored with an angel print fabric for just the right amount of holiday spirit. Fused to the quilt front, the teacups begin to dance when they're edged in a geometric swirl of binding strips. Instructions and pattern begin on page 43.

DESIGNER: MARGARET SINDELAR ● PHOTOGRAPHER: HOPKINS ASSOCIATES

Teacup Gifts

Our beautiful teacups are filled with the sweetest-ever treasures and are served up as clever gift containers. Purchase new teacups or use antique or family-heirloom china, such as these, for extra-special packaging.

PHOTOGRAPHER: HOPKINS ASSOCIATES

Baskets of Goodies

Delight Grandma or someone dear to you with a basketful of goodies that has your personal touch. Here, tucked among purchased deli items, are condiments and snacks you can put up yourself. To personalize the gift even more, line the basket with hand-decorated napkins. Recipes and instructions are on pages 44–46.

DESIGNER: CAROL DAHLSTROM ● PHOTOGRAPHER: HOPKINS ASSOCIATES

CRUMPETS

Mint Honey Jelly

Pear Raspberry

Cheese Log

Red Riding Hood Cape

Wrap your dolly this Christmas in a bright cape reminiscent of the one Little Red Riding Hood wore. Knitted in Brunswick's Liberty yarn, it's edged in seed stitches and has a latch closure at the neck. Instructions for three sizes begin on page 46.

DESIGNER: VALERIE ROOT ● PHOTOGRAPHER: HOPKINS ASSOCIATES

Red Riding Hood Topsy-Turvy Doll

Turn your little one's playtime world upside-down—then upside-down again—with the gift of a topsy-turvy doll. Utterly delightful, this moppet transforms from Red Riding Hood into Grandma with the flip of her skirt. Turn Grandma around, give her hat a lift, and it's the wolf in disguise. Instructions begin on page 47.

DESIGNER: SUSAN CAGE-KNOCH • PHOTOGRAPHER: HOPKINS ASSOCIATES

Three Christmas Pies

In that favorite poem of early childhood, **Three Little Kittens,** *the furry trio exclaims, "Oh, let us have some pie!" Your holiday guests will proclaim the same at the sight of these luscious desserts. Recipes for Key Lime, Ginger-berry, and Pecan Cream Cheese pies begin on page 54.*

PHOTOGRAPHER: HOPKINS ASSOCIATES

Soft-as-Kittens Mittens

Like the little kittens who were smitten with their mittens, these kid-size versions are "purr-fectly" suited to your little "kitties." Knitted using Superwash Bulky yarn, the pattern comes in three sizes. Make a plain set, then add duplicate-stitch designs to others. Instructions are on page 55.

DESIGNER: MARGARET SINDELAR ● PHOTOGRAPHER: HOPKINS ASSOCIATES

Gingerbread Boy Sweater

For yummy holiday outfits, sweeten purchased sweaters with gingerbread boy appliqués. Cut from suede-like fabric, the cookie figures are embellished in embroidery stitches, buttons, and bows. Try the design on other items, too, such as place mats and napkins, or a vest. Instructions and full-size pattern are on page 56.

DESIGNER: MARGARET SINDELAR ● PHOTOGRAPHER: HOPKINS ASSOCIATES

ALICE-IN-WONDERLAND ORNAMENTS

As shown on pages 20–22, ornaments measure from 5x5¼ to 7½x5 inches.

MATERIALS

for one ornament

FABRICS

8x10-inch piece of 14-count white Aida cloth

5x6-inch piece of red felt

FLOSS

Cotton embroidery floss in colors listed in key

SUPPLIES

Needle

Embroidery hoop; erasable marker

6x6-inch piece of self-stick mounting board with foam

Tracing paper

Crafts knife

20-inch piece of ⅜-inch-diameter metallic-gold-and-red cord

20-inch piece of ½-inch-wide gold flat braid

20-inch piece of 1-inch-wide red pleated trim

8-inch piece of ⅛-inch-diameter red cord

Crafts glue

INSTRUCTIONS

Hem edges of fabric to prevent fraying. Find center of desired chart on *pages 36–38,* and the center of one piece of Aida cloth; begin stitching there. Use three plies of floss to work cross-stitches. Work backstitches using one ply.

Using the erasable marker, draw outline around finished piece in desired shape. Next, place tracing paper over the stitched piece and lightly trace the drawn outline; cut out tracing-paper pattern. Place tracing-paper pattern on mounting board; trace around shape. Cut out mounting board shape with a crafts knife. Cut matching back from felt.

Add a 1-inch seam around the drawn outline of the stitched piece; cut out shape. Peel the protective paper from the mounting board. Center the foam side of the

ALICE-IN-WONDERLAND ORNAMENTS

ANCHOR		DMC		ANCHOR		DMC	
002	⊡	000	White	136	◆	799	Medium Delft blue
1006	◪	304	Medium Christmas red	359	●	801	Medium coffee brown
403	■	310	Black	130	▽	809	True Delft blue
9046	▼	321	True Christmas red	043	⋈	815	Medium garnet
008	♡	353	Dark peach	277	⌗	831	True bronze
401	⊕	413	Dark pewter	907	⊡	832	Medium bronze
398	▷	415	Light pearl gray	907	✳	833	Light bronze
310	◢	434	Medium chestnut	945	╱	834	Pale bronze
1045	⊞	436	Dark tan	881	▬	945	Dark ivory
1005	△	498	Dark Christmas red	1010	⊠	951	Medium ivory
923	◀	699	Dark Christmas green	**BACKSTITCH**			
227	○	701	True Christmas green	403	╱	310	Black– around black areas, Mad Hatter's hat, tie, shoes; Rabbit's eye, clock hands, numerals; Queen's hair, hearts on skirt and bodice; Dee and Dum's eyes, shirt, ties, pants; Alice's shoes
238	✳	703	True chartreuse				
256	☆	704	Light chartreuse				
361	▯	738	Light tan				
234	◺	762	Pale pearl gray	382	╱	3371	Black brown– all ornaments
133	◉	796	Medium royal blue				
131	★	798	Dark Delft blue				

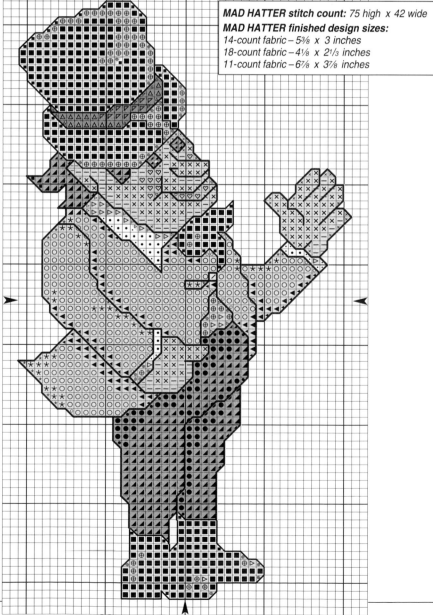

MAD HATTER stitch count: *75 high x 42 wide*
MAD HATTER finished design sizes:
14-count fabric – 5⅜ x 3 inches
18-count fabric – 4⅛ x 2⅓ inches
11-count fabric – 6⅞ x 3⅞ inches

MAD HATTER

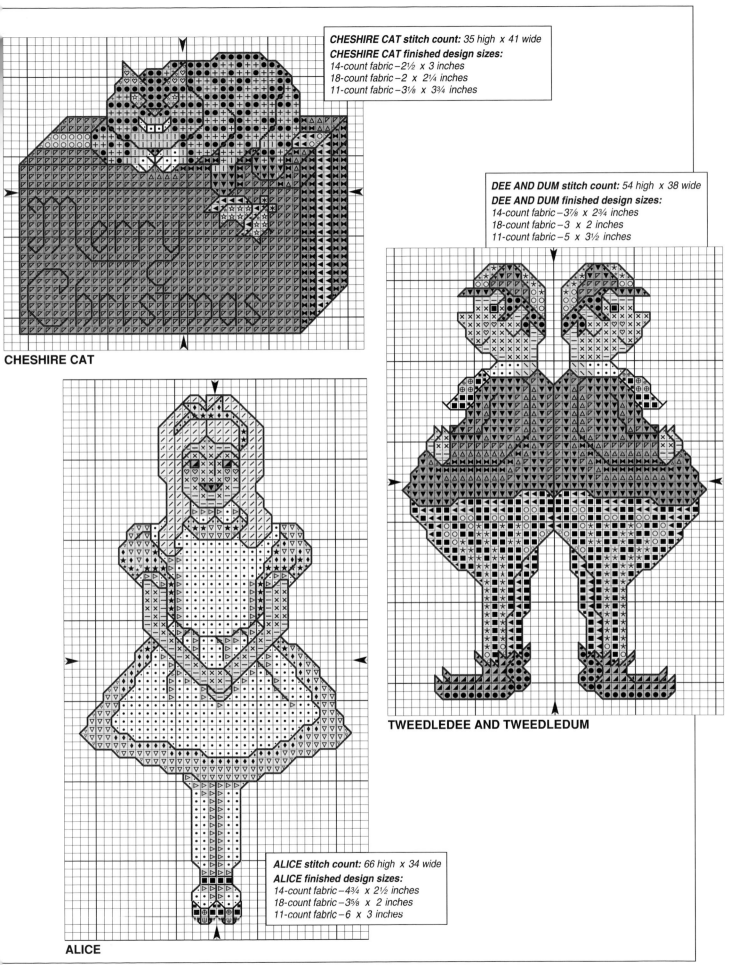

CHESHIRE CAT stitch count: *35 high x 41 wide*
CHESHIRE CAT finished design sizes:
14-count fabric – 2½ x 3 inches
18-count fabric – 2 x 2¼ inches
11-count fabric – 3⅛ x 3¾ inches

DEE AND DUM stitch count: *54 high x 38 wide*
DEE AND DUM finished design sizes:
14-count fabric – 3⅞ x 2¾ inches
18-count fabric – 3 x 2 inches
11-count fabric – 5 x 3½ inches

CHESHIRE CAT

TWEEDLEDEE AND TWEEDLEDUM

ALICE stitch count: *66 high x 34 wide*
ALICE finished design sizes:
14-count fabric – 4¾ x 2½ inches
18-count fabric – 3⅝ x 2 inches
11-count fabric – 6 x 3 inches

ALICE

37

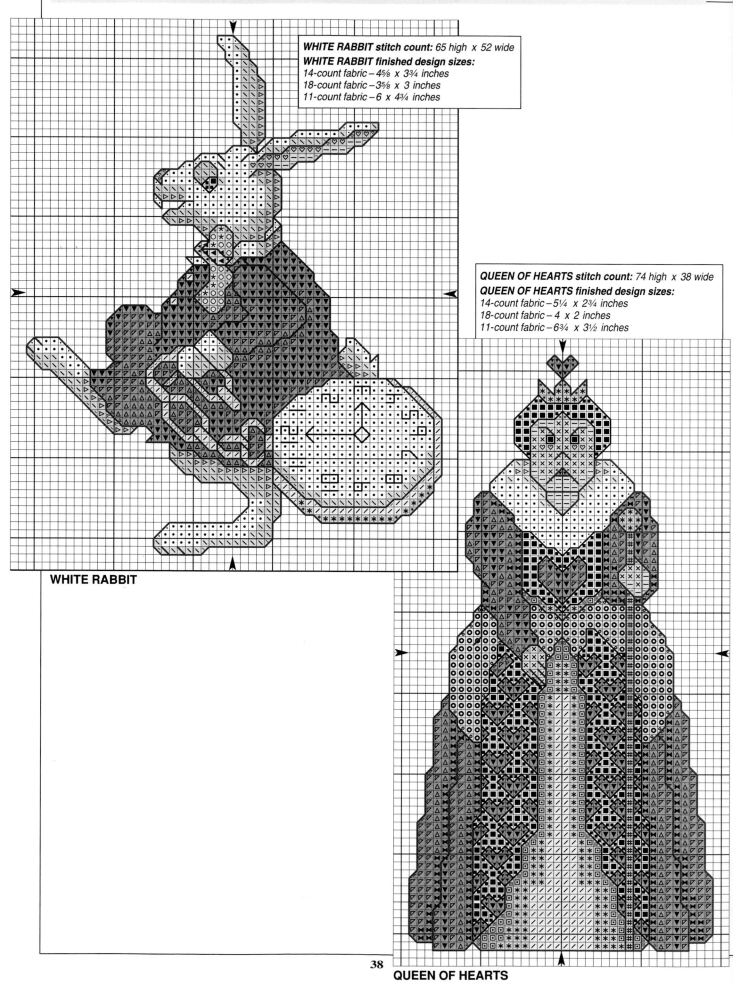

WHITE RABBIT stitch count: 65 high x 52 wide
WHITE RABBIT finished design sizes:
14-count fabric – 4⅝ x 3¾ inches
18-count fabric – 3⅝ x 3 inches
11-count fabric – 6 x 4¾ inches

QUEEN OF HEARTS stitch count: 74 high x 38 wide
QUEEN OF HEARTS finished design sizes:
14-count fabric – 5¼ x 2¾ inches
18-count fabric – 4 x 2 inches
11-count fabric – 6¾ x 3½ inches

WHITE RABBIT

QUEEN OF HEARTS

mounting board on the back of the stitched design and press. Fold raw edges of Aida cloth to the back; glue in place, clipping into the seam allowance as needed.

Glue gold-and-red cord around edge of ornament, overlapping ends at bottom. Glue gold braid behind cord; glue pleated trim around ornament behind gold braid. For hanger, fold red cord in half. Glue ends to top center of ornament. Glue felt to back of ornament.

ALICE-IN-WONDERLAND PLAYING CARD GARLAND

As shown on pages 20–22.

MATERIALS
**Two or three decks of playing cards
5 or 6 yards of narrow ribbon**

INSTRUCTIONS
Punch a hole on each side of the playing cards, placing holes about one-third of the way down from the top edge of the cards.

Loosely thread ribbon through holes as follows: Leaving a 6-inch tail at the beginning and end of the garland, thread ribbon through hole from the front of one card to the back, across the back, then up through the hole to the front.

Continue adding cards in same manner until desired length is achieved. Tie bows on each end.

CHRISTMAS TEA COZY

As shown on page 23, finished cozy measures 9x11 inches.

MATERIALS
**Tracing paper; adhesive tape
Tissue paper
½ yard of 45-inch-wide ivory wool gabardine fabric
Lightweight fusible interfacing
Dressmaker's carbon paper
Cotton embroidery floss: Christmas green (DMC 701) and red (DMC 321)
Tapestry needle
3 yards of 4-millimeter-wide iridescent ivory silk embroidery ribbon
6 yards of 4-millimeter-wide pink silk embroidery ribbon
6 yards of 4-millimeter-wide red silk embroidery ribbon
3 yards of 2-millimeter-wide gold silk embroidery ribbon
6 yards of 7-millimeter-wide mauve silk embroidery ribbon
6 yards of 7-millimeter-wide forest green silk embroidery ribbon
½ yard of fleece
Ivory sewing thread
½ yard of 45-inch-wide ivory cotton batiste lining
1 yard of narrow piping cord
Fabric glue
2 yards of ¾-inch-wide ivory-with-metallic-gold flat braid**

INSTRUCTIONS
Trace embroidery pattern, *page 40,* onto tracing paper; set aside.

Tape two pieces of tissue paper together along top and sides (pieces should be large enough to easily slip over teapot). Slide taped shape over teapot. Referring to the photograph, *page 23,* cut a curved top, allowing plenty of space all around. Refine and retape pattern as necessary. Slide shape over teapot once more to check fit.

Separate the pieces of the tissue-paper shape; discard one. Use the other piece to trace shape onto tracing paper; add ½-inch seam allowances all around. Set pattern piece aside.

Cut two rectangles from gabardine larger than the pattern. Following manufacturer's instructions, iron interfacing to the twill side of each gabardine rectangle.

Transfer the embroidery pattern to the center right side of one gabardine rectangle using dressmaker's carbon paper (this is the cozy front).

Embroider the design as follows: Backstitch the letters and stem-stitch the branches using three plies of green embroidery floss; work scroll accents using split stitches and iridescent ivory ribbon; work lazy daisy stitches, as indicated, for poinsettias using pink ribbon; add one or two red ribbon lazy daisy stitches between each pink one to fill in the flowers, and work several gold ribbon French knots for the flower centers. Make the base for each spider-web rose using straight

CHRISTMAS
TEA COZY

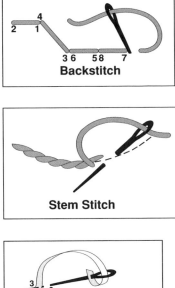

Backstitch

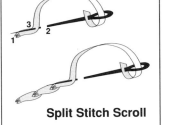

Stem Stitch

Split Stitch Scroll

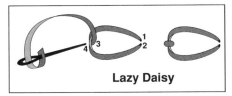

Lazy Daisy

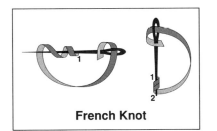

French Knot

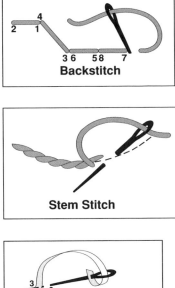

Japanese Leaf Stitch

TEA COZY
BACKSTITCH
/ Green floss – lettering
STEM STITCH
/ Green floss – branches
SPLIT STITCH SCROLL
/ 4mm Iridescent yellow ribbon
LAZY DAISY
⬧ 4mm Pink ribbon
⬧ 4mm Red ribbon
FRENCH KNOT
⬤ 2mm Gold ribbon
⬤ 4mm Pink ribbon
⬤ 4mm Red ribbon
STRAIGHT STITCH (base of roses)
✗ Red floss
JAPANESE LEAF STITCH
⬤ 7mm Forest green ribbon

---

stitches and six plies of red embroidery floss in the configuration shown on *page 40*. Work the top two large roses using mauve ribbon. Begin the bottom large rose using red ribbon, and finish it using the mauve ribbon. Work the small roses within the letters using red ribbon.

Embroider each leaf using forest green ribbon and Japanese leaf stitches. Add red and pink French knots to branches at dots.

Layer fleece behind each gabardine rectangle; baste. Machine-quilt the plain rectangle (this is the cozy back).

Center the tissue-paper pattern over stitching on cozy front. Draw around pattern; cut out. In addition, use pattern to cut out cozy back from the quilted rectangle and two lining pieces from batiste.

Sew all seams with right sides of fabric facing using ½-inch seam allowances, unless otherwise indicated. After stitching, trim seam allowances and clip curves.

Cut piping cord to fit around curved edge of cozy front. Cut 1½-inch-wide bias strips from gabardine; join short ends to make strip slightly longer than the cord. Cover cord with gabardine strip to make piping. Sew piping to cozy front, matching raw edges.

For hanging loop, join long edges of a ½x3-inch gabardine strip, using a ¼-inch seam. Turn right side out. Stitch ends side by side at top center of cozy front, matching raw edges.

Sew cozy front to back along piping sewing line; do not turn right side out. Sew lining front to back in the same manner; turn lining right side out. Slip lining inside cozy so the right sides are facing. Sew lining to the cozy around the bottom edge, leaving an opening for turning. Trim seam, turn cozy right side out, then sew the opening closed. Carefully press around the bottom edge only.

Topstitch ¼ inch from the bottom edge. Glue braid around curved edge behind piping and around the bottom edge.

CURRANT-ORANGE SCONES
Pictured on page 24.

INGREDIENTS
1   package piecrust mix
    (for 2-crust pie)
1   tablespoon sugar
1   teaspoon finely shredded
    orange peel
1½ teaspoons baking powder
⅛ teaspoon baking soda
½ cup buttermilk or sour milk*
½ cup currants or chopped
    raisins

METHOD
Combine the buttermilk and currants or chopped raisins in a small mixing bowl; let stand for 5 minutes. Meanwhile, stir together piecrust mix, sugar, orange peel, baking powder, and baking soda in a medium mixing bowl. Make a well in the center. Add buttermilk mixture to dry ingredients all at once.

Using a fork, stir just till dough clings together. (The dough will be sticky.)

On a well-floured surface, knead dough gently for 10 to 12 strokes. Roll or pat into an 8-inch circle; cut into 8 or 10 wedges.

Transfer to a lightly greased baking sheet, allowing space between the wedges. Bake, uncovered, in a 425° oven for 12 to 15 minutes or till golden. Serve warm. Makes 8 or 10 scones.

Note: To make sour milk, add milk to 1½ teaspoons lemon juice to equal ½ cup. Let stand for at least 5 minutes.

CHOCOLATE-TRUFFLE TARTS

Pictured on page 24.

INGREDIENTS

½   of an 11-ounce package piecrust mix or 1 stick piecrust mix
¼   cup finely chopped pecans or hazelnuts
2   tablespoons sugar
4   ounces semisweet chocolate
¼   cup whipping cream
3   tablespoons butter or margarine
1   beaten egg yolk
2   tablespoons desired liqueur or whipping cream
⅓   cup white baking pieces with cocoa butter, melted (optional)
Fresh fruits (such as raspberries or cherries), fruit preserves, nuts, or edible flowers (such as violas)

METHOD

Prepare piecrust mix according to package directions, *except* add the ¼ cup nuts and the sugar to the dry mix. Shape into twenty-four ¾-inch balls.

Press into bottom and up sides of 24 ungreased 1¾-inch muffin cups. Bake in a 450° oven for 6 to 8 minutes or till edges begin to brown. Cool in pans on a wire rack. Remove from pans.

For filling, in a heavy saucepan combine chocolate, ¼ cup whipping cream, and butter or margarine. Cook and stir over low heat till chocolate is melted. Gradually stir about *half* of the hot mixture

into the egg yolk. Return all of the mixture to the saucepan. Cook and stir just till mixture starts to bubble. Remove from heat.

Stir in liqueur. Transfer chocolate mixture to a small bowl; chill for 1½ to 2 hours or till mixture is cool and smooth, stirring occasionally. (The butter may separate but will blend in when the mixture is stirred.)

Beat the chilled chocolate mixture with an electric mixer on medium speed about 2 minutes or till light and fluffy. If desired, spoon the chocolate mixture into a decorating bag fitted with a large star tip (about ½ inch opening). Pipe or spoon the mixture into the baked tart shells. Cover and chill for up to 24 hours.

Before serving, let stand at room temperature for 15 to 20 minutes. If desired, drizzle tarts with white chocolate and top with fruits, preserves, nuts, or edible flowers. Makes 24 tarts.

MINI-BAGELS WITH HAM AND LEMON-CAPER CREAM

Pictured on page 25.

INGREDIENTS

⅓   cup mayonnaise or salad dressing
1   tablespoon capers, drained
½   teaspoon finely shredded lemon peel
½   teaspoon Dijon-style mustard
⅛   teaspoon white pepper
9   Mini-bagels, halved Lettuce leaves or curly endive
8   ounces ham or smoked turkey, thinly sliced

METHOD

Stir together the mayonnaise or salad dressing, drained capers, shredded lemon peel, Dijon-style mustard, and white pepper in a small mixing bowl.

Line mini-bagels with lettuce leaves or curly endive.

Using 8 ounces total, arrange thinly sliced ham or smoked turkey on lettuce.

Top with 1 teaspoon of the mayonnaise mixture. If desired, garnish with fresh dill. Serve at once. Makes ⅓ cup (18 servings).

PINEAPPLE-CARROT TEA BREAD

Pictured on page 24.

INGREDIENTS

2¼   cups all-purpose flour
1   package active dry yeast
1   8-ounce can crushed pineapple (juice pack)
¼   cup sugar
¼   cup margarine or butter
½   teaspoon salt
1   egg
1   teaspoon vanilla
½   cup shredded carrot

METHOD

Lightly grease an 8x4x2-inch loaf pan; set aside. In a large mixing bowl stir together ¼ *cup* of the flour and the yeast; set aside.

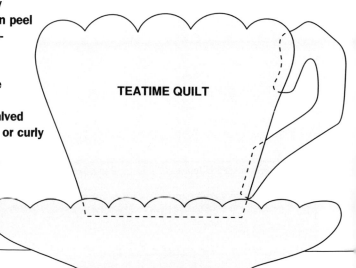

TEATIME QUILT

Drain the pineapple, reserving $1/3$ cup of the juice. In a saucepan, heat and stir reserved pineapple juice, sugar, margarine or butter, and salt just till warm (120° to 130°) and the margarine is almost melted. Add to flour mixture.

Add egg and vanilla. Beat with an electric mixer on low to medium speed for 30 seconds, scraping bowl occasionally. Beat on high speed for 3 minutes.

Stir in pineapple and carrot. Using a spoon, stir in remaining flour (batter will be sticky).

Spoon the batter into prepared pan. Cover and let rise in a warm place till almost double (45 to 60 minutes). Bake in a 375° oven for 35 to 40 minutes or till golden, covering with foil the last 10 minutes, if necessary. Remove bread from pan. Cool on wire rack. Makes 1 loaf (16 servings).

TORTILLA ROLL-UPS WITH HONEY-VEGETABLE VINAIGRETTE
Pictured on page 25.

INGREDIENTS
- **1** tablespoon salad oil
- **1** tablespoon vinegar
- **1** tablespoon honey
- **1** teaspoon course-grain brown mustard
- **1½** cups Chinese cabbage, chopped
- **½** cup shredded carrot
- **12** 6-inch flour tortillas
- **Boston lettuce leaves**

METHOD
Warm the tortillas by placing in tin foil in a 350° oven for about 10 minutes or till heated through.

Meanwhile, stir together salad oil, vinegar, honey, and brown mustard in a medium mixing bowl. Add chopped Chinese cabbage and shredded carrot; toss gently to coat.

Place the lettuce leaves atop each warm tortilla. Spoon about *2 tablespoons* cabbage mixture atop each tortilla.

Roll up jelly-roll style; slice the roll into 1-inch-thick pinwheels. Makes about 1½ cups of filling (about 7 appetizers).

TEATIME QUILT
As shown on page 26, the quilt measures 16x19 inches.

MATERIALS
½ yard of 45-inch-wide medium green print fabric
½ yard of 45-inch-wide light blue plaid fabric
¼ yard each of two different 45-inch-wide rose prints
¼ yard of 45-inch-wide light yellow fabric
Tracing paper
Paper-backed iron-on adhesive
Gold metallic machine-embroidery thread
Erasable marker; ruler; straight pins
16x19-inch piece of cotton batting
Light blue and rose sewing threads

INSTRUCTIONS
Wash, dry, and press all fabrics. From green print, cut two 16x19-inch rectangles for quilt top and back. From light blue plaid, cut ½-inch-wide bias strips; join ends to make a long strip measuring about 9 feet long. From one rose print, cut two 2½x18-inch strips and two 2½x21-inch strips for binding. From light yellow, cut six 3¼x4¼-inch rectangles for blocks.

For blocks, trace three parts of teacup pattern, *opposite,* onto tracing paper; cut out. Draw around pattern onto paper side of paper-backed adhesive six times (for six teacups).

Following the manufacturer's instructions, fuse paper-backed adhesive to remaining rose print.

TEATIME QUILT

5"
5"   6"
4½"

43

Cut out teacup pieces, remove adhesive paper backing, and fuse complete teacup to center of each yellow block. Machine-satin-stitch teacup edges using gold metallic thread. Fuse paper-backed adhesive to back of each block. Referring closely to pattern and measurements shown for placement, remove paper backing and fuse blocks to quilt top.

Press under ⅛ inch along each long raw edge of blue plaid bias strip so strip measures ¼ inch wide. Use erasable marker and ruler to draw guide lines on quilt top for bias strip placement as shown on pattern, *page 43*. Pin bias strips along guidelines, cutting lengths as necessary. Begin and end strips beyond the binding seam line. At points of crossing, weave strips through each other as they cross. When correctly positioned, slip-stitch all strips to quilt. If a strip buckles where it turns a sharp angle, tack it down with tiny stitches.

Layer the quilt top, batting, and backing. Baste all pieces together, working from the center outward in a spoke pattern. Machine-quilt around the green print shapes, using the gold metallic thread; quilt close to the bias-strip edges. Remove the basting threads.

Press under ¼ inch along both raw edges of each quilt-binding strip. With fold along binding seam line and right sides facing, sew binding strips in place. Sew the longer strips to the long sides and the shorter strips to the short sides through all layers. Turn strips to back, mitering corners and trimming ends as necessary. Turn under ¼ inch along raw edges; slip-stitch to quilt back.

HOT FUDGE SAUCE

Pictured on page 28.

INGREDIENTS
- 32 ounces semisweet chocolate
- 2½ cups half-and-half or light cream
- 1¾ cups sugar
- 1 teaspoon vanilla

METHOD

Combine semisweet chocolate, half-and-half or light cream, and sugar in a 4-quart Dutch oven or large saucepan. Bring to boil; reduce heat. Simmer mixture, uncovered, over low heat till creamy (about 2 minutes); stir frequently. Remove from heat; stir in vanilla.

Pour hot sauce into seven hot, clean half-pint jars or fourteen 4-ounce jars, leaving a ½-inch head space. Place metal lids on jars. Screw metal bands onto jars following manufacturer's directions.

Store chocolate sauce in refrigerator for up to 3 weeks. (Mixture will thicken as it chills.)

Serve sauce warm over ice cream, cream puffs, or fresh berries. (To reheat, place ½ cup sauce in a 1-cup glass measure. Micro-cook, uncovered, on 100% power [high] for 1½ to 2 minutes or till heated through, stirring once. Or, place sauce in small saucepan. Cook and stir over medium heat just till heated through.) Makes 7 half-pint or 14 half-cup jars.

Note: Sauce must be stored in the refrigerator after placing it in jars. Even though the hot sauce may cause jar lids to seal, this is not a secure canning seal. Do not store at room temperature.

MINT-HONEY JELLY

Pictured on page 29.

INGREDIENTS
- ¾ cup boiling water
- 1 tablespoon dried mint, crushed, or ¼ cup finely snipped fresh mint leaves
- 2½ cups honey
- 2 tablespoons lemon juice
- ½ of a 6-ounce package (1 foil pouch) liquid fruit pectin
- ¼ teaspoon green food coloring (optional)

METHOD

Pour boiling water over mint; let stand 5 minutes. Strain through cheesecloth-lined sieve. Measure liquid. Add enough water to measure ¾ cup. In 6-quart kettle or Dutch oven, stir together mint liquid, honey, and lemon juice.

Bring to a full rolling boil (a boil that cannot be stirred down), stirring constantly. Stir in pectin. Return to a full rolling boil. Boil hard, uncovered, 1 minute. Stir in food coloring. Skim foam.

Ladle into hot, sterilized half-pint jars, leaving ¼-inch head space. Wipe rims; adjust lids. Process in boiling-water bath 15 minutes (start timing when water boils). Makes 3 to 4 half-pints.

BLUE-CHEESE-AND-BRANDY CHEESE LOG

Pictured on page 29.

INGREDIENTS
- 2 cups shredded cheddar cheese (8 ounces)
- 1 8-ounce package cream cheese
- ½ cup crumbled blue cheese
- 3 tablespoons brandy
- 2 tablespoons finely chopped onion
- 1 tablespoon Worcestershire sauce
- Dash bottled hot pepper sauce
- Dash garlic powder
- ¼ cup snipped parsley
- ½ cup finely chopped toasted almonds
- Assorted crackers

METHOD

Bring cheddar cheese, cream cheese, and blue cheese to room temperature. In a mixer bowl beat cheeses, brandy, onion, Worcestershire sauce, hot pepper sauce, and garlic powder together with electric mixer till combined. Cover; chill for several hours or overnight. To serve, shape mixture into a log. Combine parsley and almonds. Roll cheese log in parsley-almond mixture. Serve with assorted crackers. Makes about 16 servings.

SMOKY CHEESE BALL

Pictured on page 29.

INGREDIENTS

- 1   8-ounce package cream cheese, cut up
- 1½ cups shredded smoked cheddar cheese (6 ounces)
- ½   cup shredded Swiss cheese (2 ounces)
- ½   cup margarine or butter, cut up
- 2   tablespoons dry white wine or milk
- 1   teaspoon prepared horseradish
- ½   cup finely chopped pecans or walnuts
- Assorted crackers and/or vegetables

METHOD

Bring cream cheese, cheddar cheese, Swiss cheese, and margarine or butter to room temperature.

Beat cheeses and margarine or butter in a mixer bowl with an electric mixer till combined. Beat in the wine or milk and horseradish. Cover mixture and chill for 2 hours.

Shape the cheese mixture into a large ball or two smaller balls on waxed paper. Roll balls in pecans or walnuts, pressing the nuts lightly into the balls. Wrap in clear plastic wrap.

Chill cheese ball about 3 hours or till firm. Unwrap and serve with crackers and/or vegetables. Makes 24 servings.

PEAR-RASPBERRY JAM

Pictured on page 29.

INGREDIENTS

- 6   medium pears (about 2 pounds), peeled and cored
- 1   10-ounce package frozen red raspberries (in quick-thaw pouch), thawed
- 6   cups sugar
- 2   tablespoons lemon juice
- 2   teaspoons finely shredded orange peel
- ½   of a 6-ounce package (1 foil pouch) liquid fruit pectin

METHOD

Coarsely chop pears in food processor bowl or food grinder. Add enough pears and raspberries to make 4 cups. In an 8- or 10-quart kettle of Dutch oven, mix fruit, sugar, lemon juice, and peel. Bring to a full rolling boil (a boil that cannot be stirred down), stirring constantly.

Boil hard, uncovered, for 1 minute; stir constantly. Remove from heat. Stir in pectin. Quickly skim off foam with metal spoon. Ladle jam into hot, sterilized half-pint jars; leave ¼-inch head space. Wipe rims; adjust lids. Process in boiling-water bath 15 minutes. Makes 6 to 7 half-pints.

PINEAPPLE MARMALADE

Pictured on page 29.

INGREDIENTS

- 2   large oranges
- 2   large lemons
- 1   cup unsweetened pineapple juice
- 1   20-ounce can crushed pineapple (juice pack)
- 1   1¾-ounce package powdered fruit pectin
- 5   cups sugar

METHOD

Score citrus peels into four lengthwise sections. Remove peels with a vegetable peeler. Cut into very thin strips. In medium sauce pan combine peels and pineapple juice. Bring to boiling. Cover and simmer 20 minutes; do not drain.

Cut white membrane off fruit. Section fruit over bowl to catch juices. Discard seeds. Add fruits and juices to peel mixture. Simmer, covered, 10 minutes more. Add undrained pineapple.

Transfer fruit mixture to an 8-quart Dutch oven; stir in pectin. Bring to full rolling boil, stirring constantly. Stir in sugar; return to full rolling boil. Boil hard 1 minute, stirring constantly. Remove from heat, quickly skim off foam. Ladle at once into hot sterilized half-pint jars, leaving ¼-inch head space. Wipe rims; adjust lids. Process in boiling-water bath 15 minutes (start timing when water boils). Makes 7 half-pints.

HOLLY-STAMPED NAPKIN

As shown on page 28, each holly cluster measures 2¼x1¾ inches.

MATERIALS

Fringed, ecru dinner napkin
Tracing paper; blank stamp block
Ballpoint pen
Cutting tool for cutting stamp block
Paper plate
Green and red fabric paint
Pencil with new eraser end

INSTRUCTIONS

Wash, dry, and iron napkin. Trace holly leaf pattern, *below,* onto the tracing paper and cut out. Position pattern cutout on blank stamp; draw around outline with pen. Using cutting tool, cut away area around holly leaf to make stamp.

Place center of each cluster at least 3 inches from outer edge of fringe; mark napkin with pencil dots for cluster placements as follows: Plan a cluster in each corner; center a cluster between each corner cluster; center a cluster between each of these holly clusters.

Squeeze a small amount each of red and green paint onto paper plate. For holly clusters, dip stamp into green paint, dab excess onto paper plate, then stamp three leaves with ends meeting at pencil mark. Add paint to stamp as necessary. In same manner, dip pencil eraser into red paint and stamp three berries onto center of grouping. Let dry. Iron on wrong side to set paint.

HOLLY-STAMPED NAPKIN

SNOWMAN-STAMPED NAPKIN

As shown on page 29, each snowman measures approximately 2½x3 inches.

MATERIALS
Fringed, red dinner napkin
Chalk pencil
White fabric paint
Paper plate
1¼-inch-diameter cork
1-inch-diameter cork
¾-inch-diameter cork
Black and gold paint pens

INSTRUCTIONS
Wash, dry, and iron the napkin. Plan placement of snowmen as directed for the holly napkin, *except* mark napkin with a chalk pencil and position bottom of each snowman 1¼ inches from outer edge of fringe.

Squeeze a small amount of white paint onto paper plate. Dip large cork into paint; dab cork on paper plate to remove excess paint. Stamp cork at marks on napkin, forming bottom ball of each snowman.

Use medium-size cork to stamp middle ball in place (slightly overlap bottom ball). Stamp heads with small cork (slightly overlap middle ball); let dry. Iron napkin on wrong side to set paint.

Dot eyes, nose, mouth, and buttons with black paint pen. Draw twig arms with gold paint pen.

STAR NAPKIN

As shown on pages 28–29.

MATERIALS
Fringed, green dinner napkin
Tracing paper
Paper-backed iron-on adhesive
8x12-inch piece each of three
  different yellow cotton prints

INSTRUCTIONS
Wash, dry, and iron napkin. Trace stars, *right,* onto tracing paper; cut

out. On paper-backed adhesive, draw around large star and medium stars eight times each and around the small star 11 times. Following manufacturer's instructions, fuse the large stars to the wrong side of one fabric and the remaining stars to wrong side of remaining two fabrics, mixing sizes and fabrics as desired. Cut out stars.

Remove the paper backing and arrange stars in a random pattern around the outer part of the napkin; fuse in place.

RED RIDING HOOD CAPE

As shown on page 30. Directions are for Child's Size 2. Changes for sizes 4 and 6 follow in parentheses. Finished chest size = 34 (37, 40) inches. Skill Level: Intermediate.

MATERIALS
SUPPLIES
Brunswick Liberty (3.5-ounce or
  260-yard skein): three (four, four)
  skeins of holiday red (4109)
Size 8 circular knitting needle,
  36-inch length or size needed to
  obtain gauge given below
Size 8 circular knitting needle of any
  length
Size 8 straight needles
Size H crochet hook
Two stitch holders
Two stitch markers
Two ¾-inch-diameter
  buttons

GAUGE:
In stockinette stitch, 10 sts and 13
  rows = 2 inches.

INSTRUCTIONS
In order to accommodate the large number of stitches, a circular needle is used. Work back and forth on the stitches and in rows rather than joining to work in rounds.

For cape, with circular needle, cast on 171 (185, 201) sts.

Seed St Border: P 1, * k 1, p 1; rep from * across. Work 6 more seed-st rows.

Row 8 (rs): (P 1, k 1) 3 times, k 78 (85, 93) sts, k 2 tog, k 79 (86, 94) sts, (k 1, p 1) 3 times = 170 (184, 200) sts.

Keeping first and last 6 sts at each edge in seed st, work st st (purl ws rows and knit rs rows) until piece measures 17½ (20, 22½) inches from beg, ending with a purl row and before working the seed-st border; place the 6 seed sts onto a holder to save for later.

For neck and shoulder shaping, k 2 tog across to last 6 sts; place the 6 seed sts onto a holder for later = 79 (86, 94) sts on needle. At beg of next 2 rows, bind off 2 sts = 75 (82, 90) sts. P 1 row. K across next row, dec 1 st at each edge = 73 (80, 88) sts. Work 3 rows of st st. * K 1, k 2 tog; rep from * across, ending k 1 (2, 1) = 49 (54, 59) sts. Work 5 rows of st st. Bind off 1 (2, 2) st(s), * k 2 tog and bind off, k 1 and bind off; rep from * across for 14 (15, 17) times more, bind off rem sts.

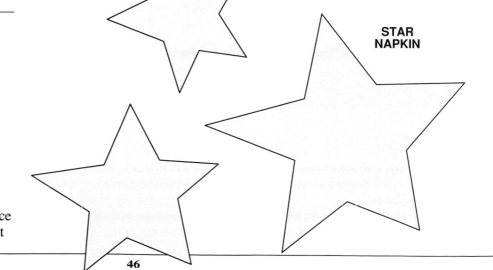

STAR NAPKIN

Hood: With the rs facing, using circular needle, and beg at right edge, work seed st across the 6 sts from holder, pick up and k 52 (56, 62) sts evenly spaced around neck edge, work seed st across 6 sts of next holder = 64 (68, 74) sts.

Row 1 (ws): Work 6 seed-st border sts, p 25 (27, 30) sts, place marker, p 2 sts, place marker, p 25 (27, 30) sts, work seed-st border on last 6 sts.

Row 2 (rs): Keeping border sts as est, k across to last st before marker, **k in front and back of next st = k-inc made,** sl marker, k 2, sl marker, k-inc, k across, ending with 6 border sts.

Rows 3–7: Keeping 6 sts along each edge in seed st for a border, work st st on center sts.

Rep rows 2–7 until there are 82 (90, 98) sts. Work even until hood measures 10 (11, 12) inches from beg, ending with a k row.

Place last 41 (45, 49) sts onto the second circular needle. Holding needles tog, begin at border edge using a straight needle and p tog the first st from each needle, k tog the next st from each needle and bind off; cont working next st from each needle tog in seed st and binding off across border sts; * p next st from each needle tog and bind off; rep from * across rem sts.

Neck latch: With straight needles, cast on 15 sts. Work 1 row of seed st.

Row 2: Inc 1 st each edge, work est pat.

Row 3: Work even. Rep rows 2 and 3 once again = 19 sts. Work est pat on first 13 sts, bind off 2 sts, work est pat to end of row. Work est pat, casting on 2 sts over the buttonhole. Dec 1 st each edge, work est pat across. Work 1 row even. Rep the last 2 rows once again = 15 sts. Work 1 row even. Bind off all sts in seed st. With rs facing and using the crochet hook, join yarn in any st along edge with a sl st; sl st evenly around and fasten off.

Finishing: Sew a button onto right neck edge between cape and hood and beside border. Insert button through neck latch. Sew second button over opposite end of latch and onto left neck edge.

RED RIDING HOOD TOPSY-TURVY DOLL

As shown on page 31, doll measures 20 inches tall.

MATERIALS
Eight tea bags
½ yard of 45-inch-wide unbleached muslin
Tracing paper
¾ yard of 45-inch-wide white calico print
⅝ yard of 45-inch-wide black-with-red print fabric
½ yard of 45-inch-wide coordinating white-with-red print fabric
⅓ yard of 45-inch-wide red fabric
Spray starch
Ecru quilting thread
Dressmaker's carbon paper
Apple Barrel acrylic paints: satin cream, nutmeg brown, black, red spice, and antique gold
Artist brushes
Small stencil brush
Threads to match fabrics
Sewing needle
Polyester fiberfill
Skein of black cotton yarn
Size 8 knitting needles
5-inch piece of cardboard
Darning needle
Crafts glue
17 inches of ¾-inch-wide red grosgrain ribbon
Natural white braided wool doll hair
2½ yards of 1-inch-wide gathered white eyelet
3¼ yards of ⅜-inch-wide white satin ribbon
Straight pins
⅔ yard of 5-inch-wide white eyelet
9½ inches of ½-inch-wide white elastic
Three ¼-inch-diameter snaps
Three small red ribbon roses
12 inches of ¼-inch-wide black satin ribbon
Fine-gauge copper wire

CENTER GUSSET OF HOOD
Cut 1
Cut 1 of lining

TOPSY-TURVY DOLL

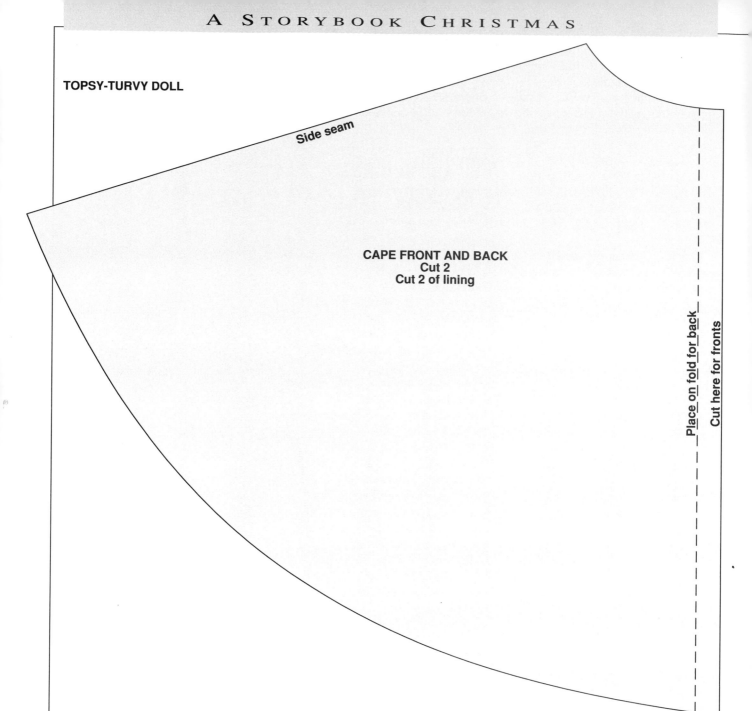

Side seam

CAPE FRONT AND BACK
Cut 2
Cut 2 of lining

Place on fold for back

Cut here for fronts

INSTRUCTIONS

Prepare a strong tea solution by steeping tea bags in ½ gallon of hot water; remove tea bags. Soak muslin in the solution until fabric is slightly darker than desired. Squeeze out excess tea. Allow fabric to dry; press.

Trace patterns, *pages 47–52,* onto tracing paper and cut out. Patterns and all measurements include ¼ inch for seam allowances. All seams are sewn with the right sides of the fabric facing, unless otherwise specified. Clip the curves as necessary.

Cut all body, head, and arm pieces from tea-dyed muslin.

Cut Granny-and-Wolf robe bodice, cuffs and sleeves from calico print. Also from calico, cut two 15-inch squares for the robe skirt and two 8¾-inch-diameter circles for the nightcap.

Cut Red Riding Hood cape lining, hood lining, collar, and cuffs from black-with-red print. Also from black-with-red print, cut the center gusset of cape hood lining and two 2½x13-inch dress flounce pieces. Cut the Red Riding Hood dress bodice, neck facing, and

sleeves from the white-with-red print. Also from the white-with-red print, cut one 13x13-inch dress skirt front and two 6x13-inch dress skirt backs.

Cut Red Riding Hood cape, cape hood, center gusset of hood and collar lining from red fabric.

Cut out the center of one nightcap circle, leaving a 1-inch-wide donut shape (this is the casing).

Lightly starch head and arm pieces. Trace face and paw details onto pattern pieces, then transfer to fabric using dressmaker's carbon paper. Transfer paw detail to oppo-

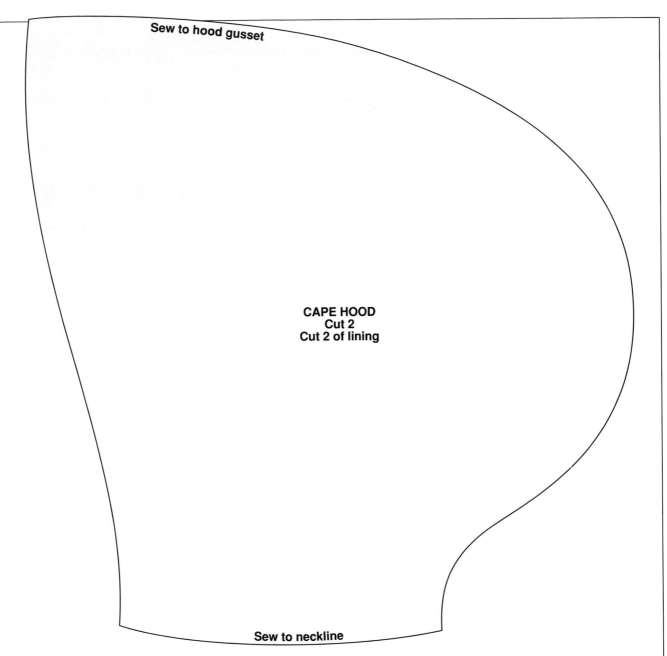

Sew to hood gusset

CAPE HOOD
Cut 2
Cut 2 of lining

Sew to neckline

site sides of only two arm pieces for Wolf left and right inner arms. Transfer Wolf tongue to one head side only.

Mix paints with water to consistency of light cream. While painting, allow each color to dry thoroughly before applying another. Paint according to instructions, below, using photograph on page 31, as a guide.

For Granny face and Red Riding Hood face, paint area around irises satin cream; paint irises and shade nose, upper lips, and eyelids with nutmeg brown; paint pupils black; and paint lips and lower eyelids red spice. Blush cheeks in a wash of red spice applied with a stencil

brush. Outline lower lips and paint nostril details, eyelashes, and eyebrows black. Use a wash of black to lightly brush in Granny wrinkles. Highlight eyes, lower lips, and noses with satin cream.

For Wolf face, paint the area around irises black; irises antique gold; and pupil, nose, paw pads, and whisker dots black.

Paint dots at eye corners and tongue red spice. Brush two ear pieces (inner ears) and cheeks with a wash of red spice. Shade tongue and paint upper eyelids black. Paint the mouth and eyebrows with a mix of nutmeg brown and black.

Using the same mixture and the stencil brush, paint in fur detail,

brushing paint over remaining ear pieces (outer ears) and along center head gusset from forehead to nose and under the chin.

Working horizontally toward back of head, brush paint along each side from just behind the ear to the chin. Using satin cream, paint teeth and highlight nose, pupils, and irises.

For Red Riding Hood, stitch head front and head back darts. Sew head back center seam from top to dot.

Join head front to one long edge of head gusset; ease to fit. Repeat for head back on other edge. Turn right side out. Press under raw edges at neck; set aside.

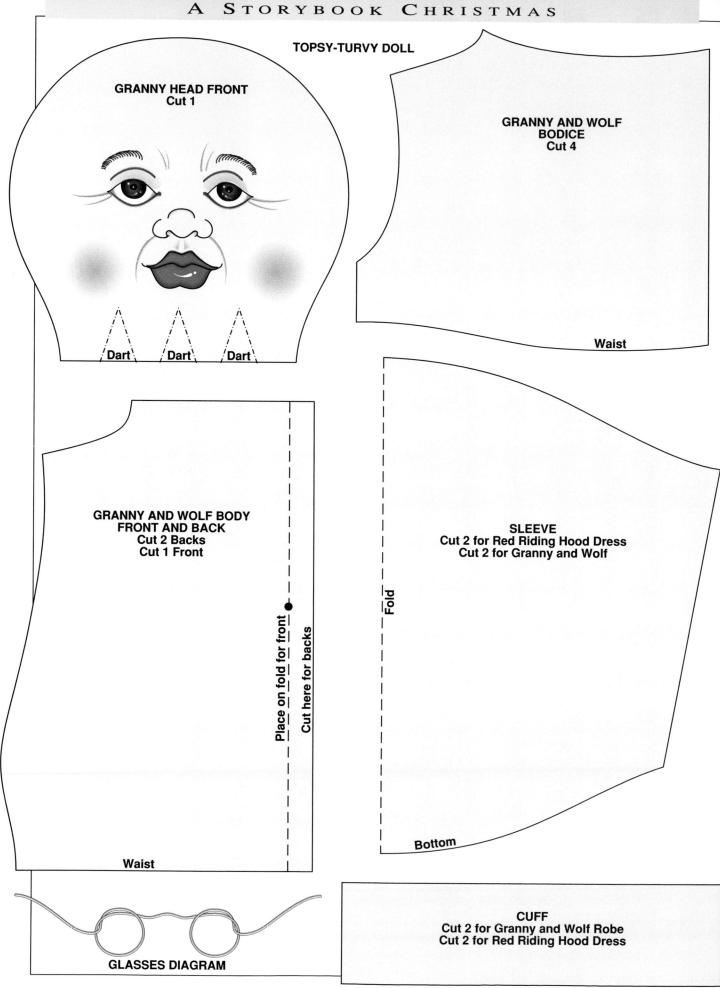

TOPSY-TURVY DOLL

GRANNY HEAD FRONT
Cut 1

Dart Dart Dart

GRANNY AND WOLF
BODICE
Cut 4

Waist

GRANNY AND WOLF BODY
FRONT AND BACK
Cut 2 Backs
Cut 1 Front

Place on fold for front

Cut here for backs

Waist

SLEEVE
Cut 2 for Red Riding Hood Dress
Cut 2 for Granny and Wolf

Fold

Bottom

GLASSES DIAGRAM

CUFF
Cut 2 for Granny and Wolf Robe
Cut 2 for Red Riding Hood Dress

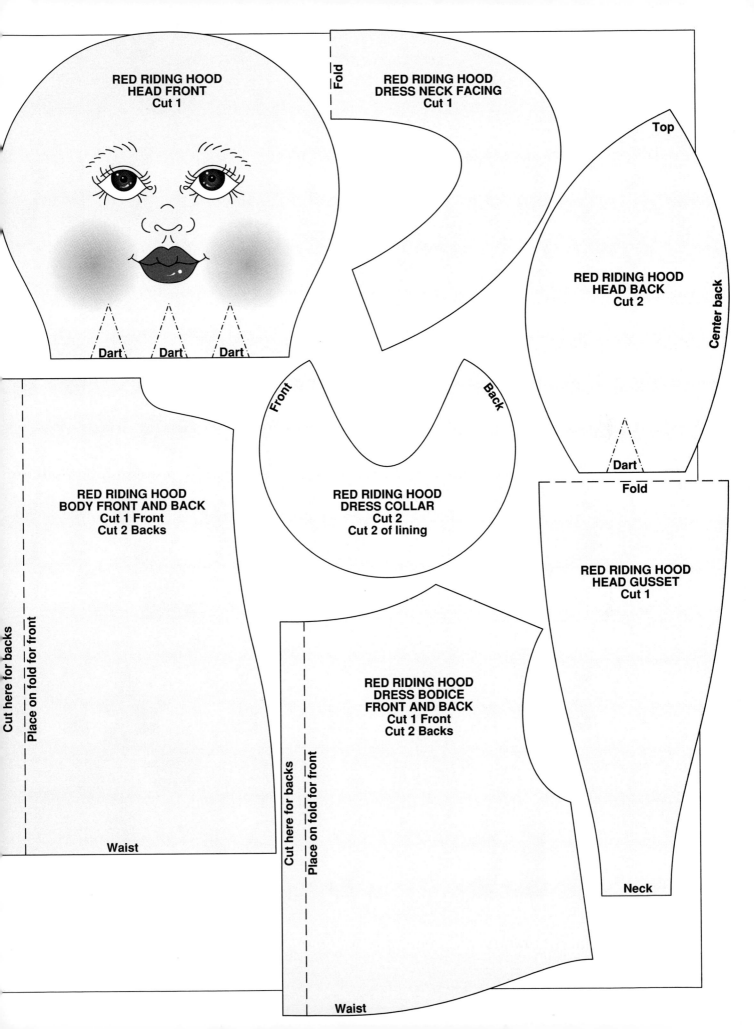

RED RIDING HOOD
HEAD FRONT
Cut 1

Dart   Dart   Dart

RED RIDING HOOD
DRESS NECK FACING
Cut 1

Fold

Top

RED RIDING HOOD
HEAD BACK
Cut 2

Center back

Front

Back

RED RIDING HOOD
BODY FRONT AND BACK
Cut 1 Front
Cut 2 Backs

Cut here for backs

Place on fold for front

Waist

RED RIDING HOOD
DRESS COLLAR
Cut 2
Cut 2 of lining

Dart

Fold

RED RIDING HOOD
HEAD GUSSET
Cut 1

RED RIDING HOOD
DRESS BODICE
FRONT AND BACK
Cut 1 Front
Cut 2 Backs

Cut here for backs

Place on fold for front

Neck

Waist

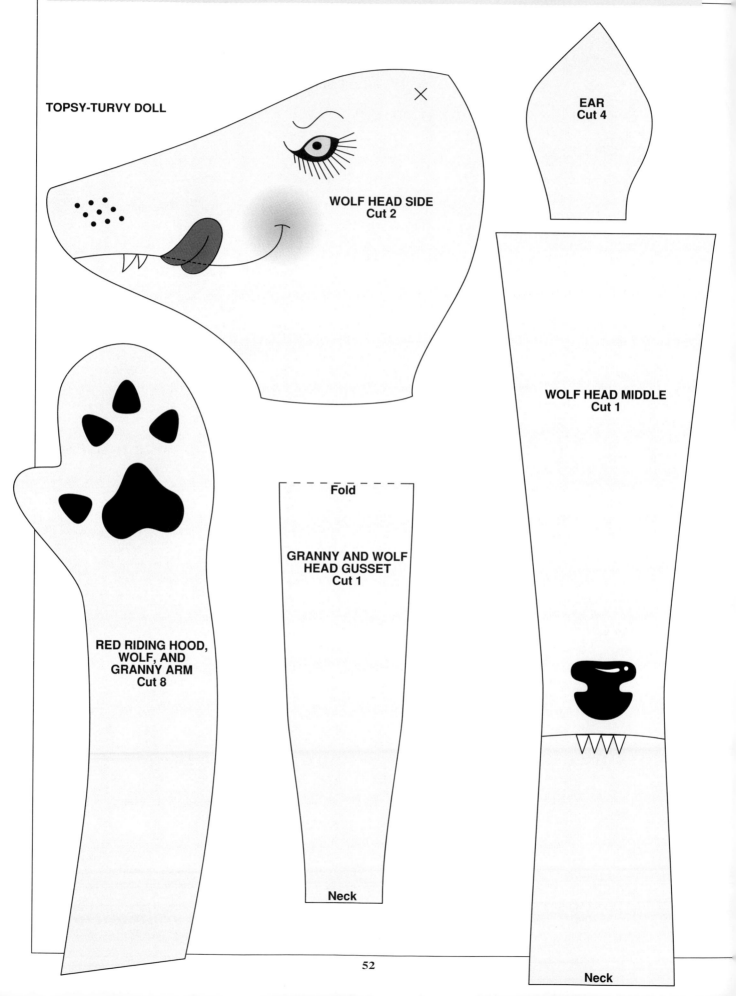

TOPSY-TURVY DOLL

EAR
Cut 4

WOLF HEAD SIDE
Cut 2

WOLF HEAD MIDDLE
Cut 1

Fold

GRANNY AND WOLF
HEAD GUSSET
Cut 1

RED RIDING HOOD,
WOLF, AND
GRANNY ARM
Cut 8

Neck

Neck

Sew the arms together in pairs, leaving the tops open. Turn the arms right side out and stuff to within ½ inch of the top. Stitch across the tops ¼ inch from raw edges. Set aside.

Baste the arms to the body front at the shoulders, matching raw edges. Sew body backs together.

Sew the body front to the body back, enclosing the arms and leaving the neck open. Matching the side seams, hand-stitch the head to the body, sewing around it twice easing to fit. Set aside.

For Granny head front, stitch darts. Sew the head front to one long edge of the Granny-and-Wolf head gusset, easing to fit. Set aside.

Sew the Wolf ears together in pairs, leaving the straight edge open for turning. Turn the ears right side out and press. Fold the ears in half lengthwise, with the inner ear to inside. Baste each folded ear to Xs on head, matching raw edges at top of the head.

Sew each Wolf head side to one long edge of the Wolf head middle piece, easing to fit. Sew Wolf head to the remaining long edge of the Granny-and-Wolf head gusset. Sew Wolf arms as for Red Riding Hood.

Stitch the Granny-and-Wolf body and sew body to head as directed for Red Riding Hood.

To assemble doll, sew Granny-and-Wolf body to the Red Riding Hood body around the waist, making tiny tucks as necessary to fit and leaving a 2-inch opening.

Turn body right side out; stuff firmly. Slip-stitch opening closed.

For Red Riding Hood hair, knit entire skein of yarn in stockinette stitch. Immerse knitted piece in boiling water for 1 hour; remove and let dry. Unravel yarn.

Wrap entire length of yarn around the cardboard. Cut along one side.

Using a darning needle threaded with a strand of yarn, sew hair to head in bunches of six strands. Begin at top gusset seam and continue tacking bunches in place until head is covered.

Trim hair as desired. Glue a bow tied from ¾-inch-wide red grosgrain ribbon to top of head.

For Granny hair, unbraid wool. Fluff wool and cut a 6½-inch length. Drape wool crosswise over head; stitch down center to make a part. Cut short bangs at top near base of part. Pull ends of wool to neck; secure with small stitches and cut off excess. Glue wool to face around hairline.

For Granny-and-Wolf robe, the front and back are identical; each has a long opening.

Sew each bodice front to bodice back at shoulders. Stitch 1-inch-wide eyelet to neck with wrong side of eyelet to right side of fabric.

Sew ⅜-inch-wide satin ribbon to neck edge along same seam line. Turn ribbon to wrong side for facing; whipstitch in place.

Gather each sleeve bottom to fit one long edge of each cuff; sew. Baste the 1-inch-wide gathered eyelet to each armhole with right sides facing.

Gather sleeve top to fit armhole; sew in place. Turn under ¼ inch at bottom edge of cuff; hem. Topstitch cuffs close to edges. Sew ⅜-inch-wide white satin ribbon around each cuff. Stitch side/sleeve seams. Set robe bodice pieces aside.

Cut each robe skirt square into one 7½x13-inch rectangle and one 6x13-inch rectangle. Matching raw edges, pin 5-inch-wide eyelet to one long edge of each 6x13-inch rectangle; place the 1-inch-wide gathered eyelet on top.

Baste eyelets to fabric. Sew each eyelet-trimmed edge to long edge of a 7½x13-inch rectangle, right sides facing. Press seams open. (Eyelet-covered area is bottom portion of robe skirt.)

Sew ⅜-inch-wide satin ribbon to each robe skirt piece ⅛ inch above the seam of the eyelet. Sew the robe skirt pieces together, sewing each seam from the bottom edge to within 3 inches from the top. (These are front and back seams.) Sew a rolled hem at the bottom.

Gather the top of each robe skirt section to fit each bodice section; stitch to bodice. Topstitch close to the seam. Turn under ¼ inch along both of the robe openings and stitch. Sew three pairs of 6-inch-long, ⅜-inch-wide white satin ribbon ties to each opening, beginning at the top and spacing them 2½ inches apart.

For Granny-and-Wolf nightcap, baste the 1-inch-wide eyelet to perimeter of the nightcap circle, matching the top edge of the eyelet with the raw edge of the fabric. Press under ¼ inch around the inner raw edge of the casing.

Stitch casing to nightcap around outer edge. Turn the casing to the inside and press. Sew the pressed edge of the casing to the nightcap, leaving an opening to insert the elastic. Insert 9½ inches of elastic through opening and sew the elastic ends together.

Sew the opening closed. Tie a bow from a 10-inch length of the ⅜-inch-wide white satin ribbon and tack to the front of the nightcap.

For Red Riding Hood dress, sew the bodice backs to the front at the shoulders. Sew each collar to a collar lining around the outer curved edge. Turn the pieces right side out and press. Baste the raw edges together on each piece.

Turn under ⅛ inch along the outer curved edge of the neck facing and stitch. With the wrong side of the collar facing the right side of bodice, sew the collar to the bodice neck.

Sew neck facing to the bodice, sandwiching collar in between. Press facing to inside; tack to shoulder seams.

Gather sleeve tops to fit armholes and stitch. Gather each sleeve bottom to fit one long edge of each cuff; stitch.

Press under ¼ inch along remaining long edges of each cuff. Turn pressed edges to inside; whipstitch to sleeve/cuff seam. Sew the side/sleeve seams.

Sew skirt backs together along long edges, stopping 5 inches from top (this is center back seam). Sew skirt front to back at sides.

Cut one skirt flounce strip in half widthwise. Sew each half to one end of remaining strip to create one long strip; press under ¼ inch twice along one long edge and stitch. Matching raw edges, baste flounce to skirt top. Trim short ends of flounce even with raw edges of skirt back.

Press under ¼ inch along the openings and stitch. Gather the skirt top to fit the bodice and stitch.

Sew three snaps to the back of the dress. Sew three evenly spaced ribbon roses to bodice front.

Sew Granny-and-Wolf robe and Red Riding Hood dress together around the bottom, leaving an opening for turning.

Turn the joined pieces right side out and press. Topstitch close to the seam on both sides.

For Red Riding Hood cape, join the cape pieces at the back seam. Repeat for lining. Join the the the cape to lining around front and the bottom edges.

Sew each cape hood piece to the hood gusset. Repeat for lining. Join the hood to the hood lining, leaving the neck edge unstitched. Turn the the hood and cape right side out and press.

Sew the hood to the cape, joining the outer fabrics only. Turn under ¼ inch on the raw edges of the hood and the cape lining; slip-stitch together.

Topstitch the cape close to the seams. Tack a 6-inch length of ¼-inch-wide black satin ribbon to each side of the front opening for the ties.

Dress the doll.

For Granny glasses, bend a 3½-inch-long piece of copper wire into the shape shown in diagram, *page 51.*

Repeat for the Wolf glasses, using a 5½-inch length of wire and making the distance between the circles longer, as necessary to go over the nose.

Bend each pair of glasses to fit the doll faces.

KEY LIME PIE

Pictured on pages 32–33.

INGREDIENTS

- **3 eggs**
- **1 14-ounce can (1¼ cups) sweetened condensed milk**
- **½ to ¾ teaspoon finely shredded Key lime peel or 1½ teaspoons finely shredded Persian lime peel**
- **½ cup water**
- **⅓ cup lime juice (8 to 10 Key limes or ⅔ Persian limes)**
- **Few drops green food coloring (optional)**
- **1 unbaked 9-inch pastry shell**
- **Meringue for Pie**

METHOD

Separate egg yolks from whites; set whites aside for meringue. For filling, in a medium mixing bowl beat egg yolks with rotary beater or fork. Gradually stir in sweetened condensed milk and lime peel. Add water, lime juice, and if desired, food coloring. Mix well. (Mixture will thicken.)

Spoon thickened filling into pastry shell. Bake in 325° oven for 30 minutes. Meanwhile, prepare Meringue for Pie as directed, *below.* Remove pie from oven. Increase oven temperature to 350°. Evenly spread meringue over hot filling. Seal to edge. Bake in 350° oven for 15 minutes or till lightly browned. Cool on a wire rack for 1 hour at room temperature. Chill 3 to 6 hours. Cover for longer storage. Makes 8 servings.

Meringue for Pie: Bring 3 *egg whites* to room temperature. In mixing bowl combine egg whites, ½ teaspoon *vanilla,* and ¼ teaspoon *cream of tartar.* Beat with electric mixer on medium speed about 1 minute or till soft peaks form (tips curl). Gradually add 6 tablespoons *sugar, 1 tablespoon* at a time, beating on high speed about 4 mintues more or till mixture forms stiff, glossy peaks and sugar dissolves. Immediately spread meringue over pie, carefully sealing

to edge of pastry to prevent shrinkage. Bake as directed in pie recipe.

GINGER-BERRY LATTICE PIE

Pictured on pages 32–33.

INGREDIENTS

- **1 15¼-ounce can crushed pineapple (juice pack)**
- **4 cups cranberries (1 pound)**
- **1¾ cups sugar**
- **¼ cup cornstarch**
- **1 to 2 tablespoons finely chopped crystallized ginger or ½ teaspoon ground ginger**
- **Pastry for Double-Crust Pie**
- **Milk**
- **Sugar**
- **Orange Cream**

METHOD

Drain pineapple, reserving 1 cup juice. (Add water if necessary to make 1 cup.) In a medium saucepan cook cranberries in reserved juice over medium high heat for 5 to 8 minutes or till cranberries begin to pop.

Combine sugar and cornstarch. Stir into hot cranberry mixture. Cook and stir till thickened and bubbly.

Remove mixture from heat. Stir in drained pineapple and ginger. Set aside to cool.

Prepare pastry. On lightly floured surface, flatten 1 ball of dough with hands. Roll from center to edge, forming a circle about 12 inches in diameter. Ease pastry into a 9-inch pie plate, being careful not to stretch. Trim to ½ inch beyond edge of pie plate.

Roll second ball of dough. Using a pastry wheel or sharp knife cut dough into ½- to ¾-inch-wide strips. Pour cranberry mixture into pasty-lined plate.

Arrange pastry strips atop filling and trim even with bottom crust. Fold the bottom pastry over thc strips and build up the edge. Seal and flute edge.

Brush pastry with milk; sprinkle with sugar. To prevent over browning, cover edge of pie with foil. Bake in 375° oven for 35 minutes. Remove foil from pie. Bake 20 to 25 minutes more or till golden. Cool on wire rack.

Serve with Orange Cream. Makes 8 servings.

Pastry for Double-Crust Pie: In mixing bowl, stir together 2 cups all-purpose *flour* and ½ teaspoon *salt*. Cut in ⅔ cup *shortening or lard* till pieces are the size of small peas. Pour 6 to 7 tablespoons *water* into a cup; sprinkle *1 tablespoon* of the water over part of mixture; gently toss with fork. Push to side of bowl. Repeat till all is moistened. Divide dough in half. Form each half into a ball.

On lightly floured surface, flatten one ball of dough with hands. Roll dough from center to edges, forming circle about 12 inches in diameter. Wrap pastry around rolling pin. Unroll onto a 9-inch pie plate. Ease pastry into pie plate (do not stretch pastry). Trim pastry even with rim of pie plate.

For top crust, roll remaining dough. Cut slits to allow steam to escape. Fill pastry in pie plate with desired filling. Place top crust on filling. Trim top crust ½ inch beyond edge of plate. Fold top crust under bottom crust; flute edge. Bake as directed.

Orange Cream: In a small mixer bowl, beat 1 cup *whipping cream* and 2 tablespoons *sugar* with an electric mixer on low speed till soft peaks form. Fold in 1 teaspoon finely shredded *orange peel*. Serve immediately.

PECAN CREAM CHEESE PIE

Pictured on page 32.

INGREDIENTS

- 2 3-ounce packages cream cheese, softened
- ½ cup sugar
- 4 eggs
- 2 teaspoons vanilla
- ¼ teaspoon salt
- 1 unbaked 9-inch pastry shell
- 1¼ cups chopped pecans
- ¾ cup light or dark corn syrup
- 3 tablespoons sugar
- 3 tablespoons margarine or butter, melted

METHOD

Place cream cheese in a medium mixing bowl. Beat with an electric mixer on medium speed till smooth. Add ½ cup sugar, 1 of the eggs, 1 teaspoon of the vanilla, and salt; beat just till combined. Spread cream cheese mixture onto the bottom of the pastry. Sprinkle pecans over the cream cheese mixture.

In a large mixer bowl, use rotary beater or whisk to lightly beat the remaining 3 eggs. Stir in the corn syrup, 3 tablespoons sugar, margarine or butter, and the remaining 1 teaspoon vanilla.

Place partially filled pastry on a baking sheet on oven rack. Slowly pour syrup mixture over pecans. Cover edge with foil. Bake in a 375° oven for 20 minutes or more, till a knife inserted near the center comes out clean. Cool pie on a wire rack. Cover and chill to store. Makes 8 servings.

SOFT-AS-KITTENS MITTENS

As shown on page 34. Directions are for children's size small, medium, and large. Skill Level: Intermediate

MATERIALS *for one pair*

Lamb's Pride Superwash Bulky (100-gram or 110-yard skein): one skein of plum crazy (SWB55), emerald city (SWB52), or romantic ruby (SWB43)

10 yards of white yarn in a bulky weight

Size 3 and 5 double-pointed knitting needles (dpn); yarn needle

Two small stitch holders; one stitch marker

GAUGE:

Working in rounds of stockinette stitch (st st) and with larger dpns, 5 sts and 7 rnds = 1 inch.

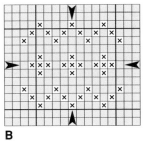

A   B

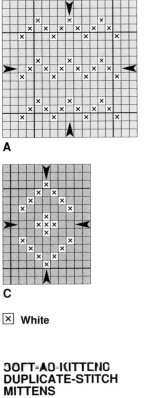

C

☒ White

SOFT-AS-KITTENS
DUPLICATE-STITCH
MITTENS

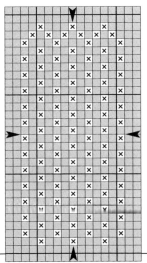

D

INSTRUCTIONS

For mittens (make two): With smaller dpns and main color, cast on 28 (32, 36) sts. Arrange the sts onto 3 dpns; join and place a marker to indicate the beginning of rnd. Work around in k 1, p 1 ribbing for 2 (2½, 2½) inches.

Change to the larger dpns. Knit every rnd for st st until the piece measures 2¾ (3½, 3½) inches from beginning.

For thumb, slip 6 sts onto holder; cast on 6 sts, k around = 28 (32, 36) sts. Work even to 4¾ (6, 6½) inches from beginning.

For shaping, Rnd 1: (K 2, k 2 tog) around. Rnd 2: K 21 (24, 27) sts. Rnd 3: (K 1, k 2 tog) around. Rnd 4: K 14 (16, 18) sts. Rnd 5: (K 2 tog) around = 7 (8, 9) sts.

Cut yarn leaving 8-inch tail. Thread tail into needle and back through remaining sts. Pull up to gather; close top opening. Secure.

To complete thumb, k 6 sts from holder, pick up and k 6 more sts around opening. Arrange the 12 sts onto 3 dpns; join. Work around in st st until thumb measures 1¼ (1½, 1¾) inches from beginning. K 2 tog around. Leaving a 6-inch tail, cut yarn. Thread tail into yarn needle and back through remaining sts. Close opening and secure in place.

Select one duplicate stitch chart, *page 55.* Count stitches on mitten top to center pattern and embroider backs with white yarn. Weave loose ends on wrong side of fabric.

GINGERBREAD BOY SWEATER

As shown on page 35.

MATERIALS

For one sweater
Tracing paper
5x12-inch piece of paper-backed iron-on adhesive
5x12-inch piece of light brown imitation suede
3x9-inch piece of red or green imitation suede

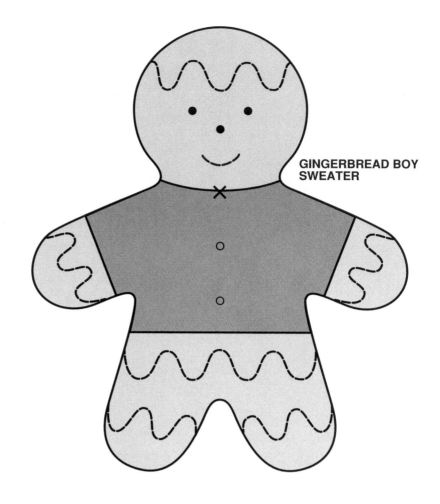

GINGERBREAD BOY SWEATER

Cotton mock turtleneck sweater in desired size and color
Press cloth; matching thread
Cotton embroidery floss: white, red, black, and green
Embroidery needle
Nine 4-millimeter black beads
8 inches of ¼-inch-wide green or red satin ribbon to contrast with red or green imitation suede
Six ½-inch acrylic star stones: two pink, two gold, and two red or green
Gem glue

INSTRUCTIONS

Trace a separate gingerbread boy and shirt pattern, from pattern *above,* onto tracing paper; cut out. Trace three gingerbread boys and three shirts onto paper side of iron-on adhesive; cut out.

Fuse gingerbread boys to brown suede and shirts to red or green suede, following the manufacturer's instructions. Cut out shapes.

Remove paper side of iron-on adhesive. Arrange gingerbread boys in a curve across top front of sweater as shown on *page 39.* Position top of the center gingerbread boy's head 2 inches below the base of the neck ribbing. Cover pieces with a press cloth; fuse in place. Position the shirts on gingerbread boys, cover with a press cloth, and fuse.

Using matching sewing thread, machine-zigzag-stitch around edges of gingerbread boys and shirts to appliqué them in place.

Referring to pattern, backstitch frosting lines using four plies of white floss and mouth using three plies of red floss. Sew bead eyes and nose in place with black floss.

Cut ribbon into three equal lengths. For each piece, fold raw edges to back. Wrap center with green or red floss to make bow. Tack bow to each gingerbread boy at neck. Glue stars to shirt at dots.

Best-Selling Bazaar

You'll be ready for the Holiday Bazaar with our collection of Christmas crafts to make in multiples and sell by the dozens. From a raggedy sweet snowman to a yummy cookie mix, these clever bazaar treats will please you and everyone at the show.

PHOTOGRAPHER: HOPKINS ASSOCIATES

Chocolate
Brownie Mix

Gumdrop Cookie M

Yummy Treats

*Working together with family and friends makes holiday cooking even more fun.
Our entire collection of yummy treats are so easy to make that you'll want to make more
than one batch. The goodies shown here are all packaged and ready to sell. Recipes and
instructions for packaging start on page 62.*

PHOTOGRAPHER: HOPKINS ASSOCIATES

Applesauce-Rhubarb Muffins

Peppery-Plum Barbecue Sauce

Peppery-Plum BBQ Sauce

Whole Wheat Pretzels

Chocolate Cashew Clusters

Elf and Reindeer Party Favors

Raggedy Snowman

Faux Cookie Ornaments

Fun Felt Santa Claus

Clever Crafts

The crafts here are so simple, you'll want to involve the whole family. Even little ones can help with this festive collection. These projects can almost be made assembly-line style so the multiples are done quicker. Instructions and patterns for all of the projects begin on page 64.

DESIGNERS: ELF AND REINDEER PARTY FAVORS, KAREN TAYLOR; RAGGEDY SNOWMAN, PAM KVITNE; FAUX COOKIE ORNAMENTS, BEV GEORGE; SNOWMAN BUTTON COVERS AND LAPEL PIN, JEFF JULSETH PHOTOGRAPHER: HOPKINS ASSOCIATES

**Snowman Button Covers
and Lapel Pin**

CHOCOLATE BROWNIE MIX

Pictured on page 58.

INGREDIENTS

- 4 cups all-purpose flour
- 1¾ cups granulated sugar
- 1 cup packed brown sugar
- ¾ cup unsweetened cocoa powder
- 2 teaspoons baking powder
- 1½ cups shortening that does not require refrigeration

METHOD

Stir the flour, sugar, brown sugar, cocoa powder, and baking powder together in a large mixing bowl. Cut in the shortening till the mixture resembles fine crumbs. Measure about 3 cups of the mixture into each of three large plastic bags. Seal each bag tightly.

Directions for the label: Place brownie mix in a large mixing bowl. In a small mixing bowl stir together 1 slightly beaten egg, and ½ cup milk. Stir into dry ingredients. (If desired, stir in ½ cup miniature semisweet chocolate pieces and/or ½ cup chopped nuts.) Spread batter evenly into a greased 9x9x2-inch baking pan. Bake in a 350° oven for 25 to 30 minutes or till a wooden toothpick inserted in center comes out clean. Cool completely on a wire rack. (Sift powdered sugar over top or frost with canned frosting, if desired.) Cut into bars. Makes 24.

GUMDROP COOKIE MIX

Pictured on page 58.

INGREDIENTS

- 1½ cups gumdrops
- 1 cup granulated sugar
- 4 cups all-purpose flour
- 1 cup packed brown sugar
- 2 teaspoons baking powder
- 1½ cups regular or butter-flavored shortening that does not require refrigeration

METHOD

Chop gumdrops into small pieces. Toss with ¼ cup of the granulated sugar, till well coated. Package one-third (about ½ cup) into each of three small plastic bags. Set aside.

Stir the flour, remaining granulated sugar, brown sugar, and baking powder together in a large mixing bowl. Cut in the shortening till the mixture resembles fine crumbs.

Measure one third of the mixture (about 2½ cups) into each of three large plastic bags. Place a bag of gumdrops on top of the flour mixture. Seal each bag tightly.

Directions for the label: In a large mixing bowl, stir together the gumdrops, cookie mix, 1 egg, and 1 teaspoon vanilla. Shape dough into 1½-inch balls. Place balls 2 inches apart on an ungreased cookie sheet. Flatten slightly with the bottom of a glass dipped in sugar. (If desired, cut decorative shapes from additional gumdrops and press lightly into cookies.) Bake in a 375° oven for 8 to 10 minutes or till bottoms are lightly browned. Remove and cool completely on wire racks. Makes about 16 cookies per bag.

Tip: If desired, reserve some of the gumdrops from the packet for decorating.

CHOCOLATE CASHEW CLUSTERS

Pictured on page 59.

INGREDIENTS

- 1 cup raisins
- 1 pound raw cashews or unsalted dry-roasted cashews or unsalted dry-roasted peanuts
- 1 pound chocolate-flavor candy coating
- Foil or paper candy cups

METHOD

Place raisins in a steamer basket. In a saucepan, place the basket over, but not touching, boiling water. Steam raisins, covered, for 5 minutes. Remove raisins from steamer basket. Let raisins stand at room temperature for 2 hours or till completely dry.

To roast raw cashews or peanuts, spread them in a shallow baking pan. Bake in a 350° oven for 15 minutes or till light brown, stirring several times. Cool cashews completely. (Omit this step if using dry-roasted cashews or peanuts.)

Melt the candy coating in a large heavy saucepan over low heat. Remove from heat.

Stir in the cashews. Add the raisins and mix well. Drop mixture by teaspoons into foil or paper candy cups or onto waxed paper. Let the candy stand in a cool, dry place till firm. Store in a tightly covered container in a cool, dry place for 2 weeks or freeze. Makes about 64 to 70 pieces.

APPLESAUCE-RHUBARB MUFFINS

Pictured on page 59.

INGREDIENTS

- 2 cups all-purpose flour
- 1 cup whole wheat flour
- 2 teaspoons baking powder
- 2 teaspoons ground cinnamon
- ½ teaspoon baking soda
- ½ teaspoon salt
- 2 eggs
- 1⅓ cups packed brown sugar
- 1⅓ cups applesauce
- ½ cup cooking oil
- 1½ cups chopped rhubarb
- Crumbled sugar cubes or cinnamon sugar

METHOD

Stir together all-purpose flour, whole wheat flour, baking powder, cinnamon, baking soda, and salt in a large mixing bowl. Make a well in center; set aside.

In a medium mixing bowl, beat eggs; stir in brown sugar, applesauce, and cooking oil. Add egg mixture all at once to flour mixture. Stir just till moistened (the batter should be lumpy). Fold in rhubarb. Make desired size muffins.

Giant Muffins: Lightly grease 3½-inch muffin cups or line with paper bake cups; fill ⅔ full. Sprinkle with sugar or cinnamon sugar. Bake in a 350° oven for 30 to 35 minutes or till tops are firm and golden. Remove from pans; serve warm. Makes 10.

Mini-Muffins: Lightly grease 1¼-inch muffin cups or line with paper bake cups; fill ⅔ full. Sprinkle with sugar or cinnamon sugar. Bake in a 400° oven for 10 to 12 minutes or till golden. Remove from pans; serve warm. Makes about 56.

Regular Muffins: Lightly grease 2¾-inch muffin cups or line with paper bake cups; fill ⅔ full. Sprinkle the tops with sugar or cinnamon sugar. Bake in a 400° oven for 18 to 20 minutes or till tops are golden. Remove muffins from pans; serve warm. Makes about 24.

Make-ahead directions: Bake muffins as directed. Cool; place in a freezer container. Freeze for up to 2 months. To serve, thaw overnight in the refrigerator or wrap in foil and heat in a 300° oven about 20 minutes or till warm.

PEPPERY-PLUM BARBECUE SAUCE
Pictured on page 59.

INGREDIENTS
2   **29-ounce cans whole unpitted purple plums**
2   **large onions, coarsely chopped (2 cups)**
4   **cloves garlic, minced**
4   **teaspoons grated fresh gingerroot**
1   **12-ounce can frozen lemonade concentrate, thawed**
⅔   **cup chili sauce**
¼   **cup prepared mustard**
2   **tablespoons Worcestershire sauce**
2   **teaspoons crushed red pepper**

METHOD
Drain one can of plums, reserving syrup in a large saucepan. Pit plums. Place plums in a blender container. Cover and blend till smooth. Add to the syrup in saucepan. Repeat with remaining plums, adding onion, garlic, and gingerroot to blender container. Cover and blend till smooth. Add to saucepan and stir in lemonade concentrate, chili sauce, mustard, Worcestershire sauce, and pepper.

Bring the mixture to boiling; reduce heat. Simmer, uncovered, for 50 to 60 minutes or till mixture is slightly thickened, stirring frequently. Ladle into hot sterilized half-pint jars, leaving ½-inch head space. Wipe rims; adjust lids. Process in a boiling-water canner for 10 minutes. Makes six 1-cup servings.

WHOLE WHEAT PRETZELS
Pictured on page 59.

INGREDIENTS
2   **to 2½ cups all-purpose flour**
1   **package active dry yeast**
1½   **cups milk**
¼   **cup packed brown sugar**
2   **tablespoons cooking oil**
1   **teaspoon salt**
2   **cups whole wheat flour**
¼   **cup chopped sunflower nuts**
1   **teaspoon salt**
3   **quarts boiling water**
1   **slightly beaten egg white**
1   **tablespoon water**
¼   **cup chopped sunflower nuts**

METHOD
Combine 1½ cups of the all-purpose flour and the yeast in a mixer bowl. In a saucepan, heat the milk, brown sugar, oil, and 1 teaspoon salt till warm (115° to 120°), stirring constantly. Add to the all-purpose flour mixture. Beat with an electric mixer on low speed for 30 seconds, scraping sides of bowl. Beat on high for 3 minutes. Use a spoon to stir in whole wheat flour,

first ¼ cup sunflower nuts, and as much of the remaining all-purpose flour as you can. Turn onto a lightly floured surface. Knead in enough of the remaining all-purpose flour to make a moderately stiff dough that is smooth and elastic (6 to 8 minutes total). Shape into a ball. Place in a lightly greased bowl; turn once. Cover and let rise till double (about 1¼ to 1½ hours).

Punch dough down. Cover and let rest for 10 minutes. On a lightly floured surface, roll the dough into a 12x10-inch rectangle. Cut into twenty 12x½-inch strips. Gently pull each strip into a rope about 16 inches long. Shape the pretzels as shown. Place on a greased baking sheet. Bake in a 475° oven for 4 minutes; remove from the oven. Reduce oven temperature to 350°.

Dissolve 1 teaspoon salt in boiling water. Lower three or four pretzels at a time into the boiling water; boil 2 minutes, turning once. Using a slotted spoon, transfer to paper towels; let stand a few seconds. Place pretzels ½-inch apart on well-greased baking sheets. Repeat with remaining pretzels.

Stir together egg white and water. Brush pretzels with mixture. Sprinkle with remianing sunflower nuts. Bake in 350° oven for 25 to 30 minutes or till brown. Remove; cool on a wire rack. Makes 20 pretzels.

Honey-Orange Pretzels: Prepare as directed except substitute orange juice for milk, honey for sugar, and omit sunflower nuts. Add ¼ cup dried currants or chopped raisins and ½ teaspoon finely shredded orange peel to the dough. Omit salt from boiling water. (Additional all-purpose flour may be needed.) If desired, sprinkle lightly with sugar before the final baking.

Buttermilk-Rye Pretzels: Prepare as directed except use 2½ to 3 cups all-purpose flour and substitute buttermilk for milk and 1½ cups rye flour for whole wheat flour. Omit sunflower nuts and add 1 tablespoon caraway seed to dough. If desired, sprinkle lightly with salt before final baking time.

RAGGEDY SNOWMAN

As shown on page 60, finished snowman is 8 inches tall.

MATERIALS

Tracing paper
2x3-inch piece of orange felt
3½x8-inch piece of dark gray wool for hat
¼ yard of white cotton sheeting
Pointed tool, such as a crochet hook or the end of a paintbrush
One 3-inch-diameter plastic-foam ball
One 2½-inch-diameter plastic-foam ball
One 2-inch-diameter plastic-foam ball
Six toothpicks
Crafts glue
10 assorted black shank buttons, with diameters ranging from ¼- to ⅜-inch-wide
Sewing threads to match the fabrics
¼x12-inch piece of cotton check for the scarf
Two 3½-inch-long tree twigs for the arms

INSTRUCTIONS

Trace the patterns, *below,* onto the tracing paper and cut out. Patterns include ¼ inch for the seam allowances.

Cut the nose from orange felt and the hat from gray wool. Set the pieces aside.

Tear white cotton sheeting into fifteen ¾-inch-wide strips. Cut the strips into 1-inch-long pieces. Position the end of the pointed tool in the center of each piece and press ⅛ inch deep into the plastic-foam balls. Cover balls entirely with pieces spaced ¼ inch apart.

For snowman bottom, flatten one side of the largest ball by pressing hard against a flat surface.

Join the balls by inserting three toothpicks into the top of the largest ball as follows: Position toothpicks ¼ inch apart in a triangular configuration and push each halfway into the ball.

Add a drop of glue to each toothpick and press the medium ball onto the toothpicks. Repeat the procedure to join the small ball to the medium ball.

Glue two black shank buttons to the medium ball for buttons. For the face, glue black shank button eyes in place; use five black shank buttons for the mouth.

For the hat, sew circles together with right sides facing, leaving an opening as noted on the pattern. Trim the seam, clip the curve, and turn right side out through the opening. Press, then slip-stitch the opening closed.

Sew the remaining black button to the center top of the hat. Glue the hat to the head.

For the nose, sew side edges together, leaving the base open. Trim seam and turn right side out. Attach nose to head by pressing open edge into the head, using the pointed tool; secure with glue.

Tie scarf around snowman's neck. Press twigs into body for arms and secure with glue.

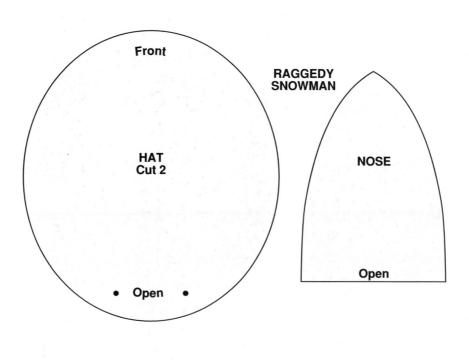

Front

RAGGEDY SNOWMAN

HAT
Cut 2

Open

NOSE

Open

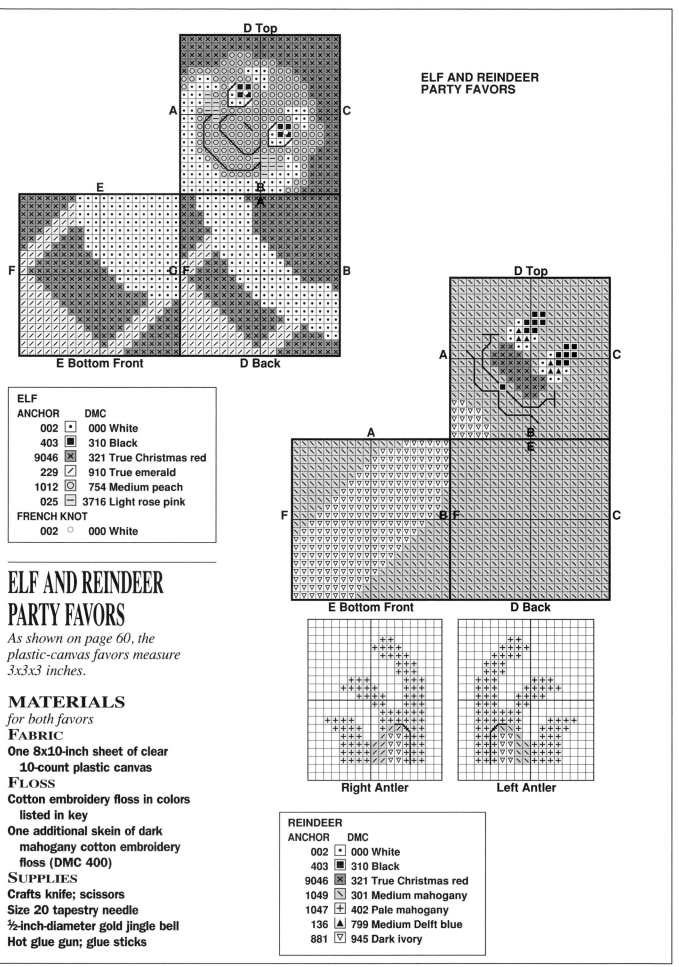

D Top

A **C**

**ELF AND REINDEER
PARTY FAVORS**

E

F **G F** **B**

E Bottom Front **D Back**

ELF

ANCHOR		DMC
002	•	000 White
403	■	310 Black
9046	⊠	321 True Christmas red
229	⁄	910 True emerald
1012	○	754 Medium peach
025	–	3716 Light rose pink
FRENCH KNOT		
002	○	000 White

ELF AND REINDEER PARTY FAVORS

As shown on page 60, the plastic-canvas favors measure 3x3x3 inches.

MATERIALS

for both favors

FABRIC

One 8x10-inch sheet of clear 10-count plastic canvas

FLOSS

Cotton embroidery floss in colors listed in key

One additional skein of dark mahogany cotton embroidery floss (DMC 400)

SUPPLIES

Crafts knife; scissors

Size 20 tapestry needle

½-inch-diameter gold jingle bell

Hot glue gun; glue sticks

D Top

A **C**

A

B
E

F **B F** **C**

E Bottom Front **D Back**

Right Antler **Left Antler**

REINDEER

ANCHOR		DMC
002	•	000 White
403	■	310 Black
9046	⊠	321 True Christmas red
1049	⟍	301 Medium mahogany
1047	+	402 Pale mahogany
136	▲	799 Medium Delft blue
881	▽	945 Dark ivory

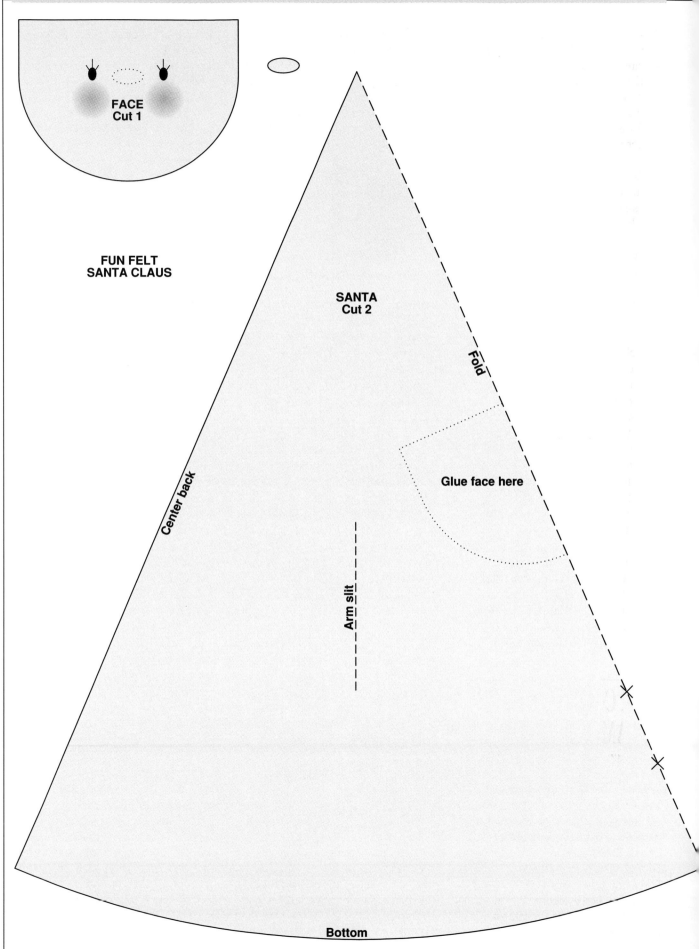

FACE
Cut 1

FUN FELT
SANTA CLAUS

SANTA
Cut 2

Fold

Center back

Glue face here

Arm slit

Bottom

INSTRUCTIONS

For each party favor, cut three squares of plastic canvas measuring 21x21 holes. For the reindeer antlers, cut two pieces of plastic canvas measuring 20x15 holes.

For each square and antler, find center of chart, *page 65,* and plastic canvas; begin stitching there.

Use a doubled six-ply strand of cotton embroidery floss to work half cross-stitches coming up in the bottom left corner and going down in the upper right corner.

Use six plies of black embroidery floss to work backstitches on the elf and reindeer face. Work the backstitches on the reindeer antlers using six plies of dark mahogany (DMC 400) embroidery floss. Add the French knot highlights to each of the elf's eyes using six plies of white embroidery floss.

When all of the pieces are stitched, whipstitch the edges marked A and B on the key, using embroidery floss to match the stitches.

Whipstitch the squares together, matching the lettered sides as shown on the key. Use floss to match the stitches and leave the previously whipstitched edges unjoined. Tack a jingle bell to the top of the elf's head.

Trim the plastic canvas carefully around the stitching on the antlers. Whipstitch the edges all around, using a six-ply strand of matching embroidery floss. Hot-glue the antlers in place at the top of the head.

FAUX COOKIE ORNAMENTS

As shown on page 60.

MATERIALS

Simple outline cookie cutters such as trees, gingerbread boys, stars, etc.
Sheets of ½-inch-thick plastic foam
Pale yellow napkins
Toothpicks; Modge Podge
Small sponge
Ochre and burnt sienna acrylic paints
Fabric paint pens in desired colors
Crystal fabric glitter

INSTRUCTIONS

For each ornament, push a cookie-cutter shape into and all the way through the plastic-foam sheet; release the cookie shape.

Turn the shape over so the top has a rounded, more irregular outline. Brush away any of the loose plastic-foam particles.

Round the top edge and make slight indentations in the top of the surface, using your fingers, to texture the cookie.

Separate the napkin plies and tear them into pieces slightly larger than the ornament. Holding the ornament on a toothpick, brush the top and sides with Modge Podge using the small sponge.

Cover the wet ornament with one layer of napkin. Smooth the napkin over the surface. Bush the edges with another coat of Modge Podge.

In the same manner, coat the back side of the ornament. Stick the toothpick holding the ornament into the plastic-foam scrap.

Pierce a hole at the top of the ornament to receive a hanging loop. Allow the piece to dry.

Lay the ornament flat and decorate with fabric paints, as desired or referring to photo on page 60 for ideas. Then, while the paint is still wet, sprinkle the ornament with crystal fabric glitter. Allow cookie ornament to dry.

Lightly brush away any excess glitter. Use a narrow piece of ribbon or monofilament for hanging loop.

FUN FELT SANTA CLAUS

As shown on page 61, Santa is 14 inches tall.

MATERIALS

Tracing paper
Four 9x11-inch rectangles of red felt for body
4x8-inch piece of black felt for boots
4x7-inch piece of green felt for mittens
2x3-inch piece of ecru felt for face
2½x45-inch strip of white diaper flannel
One 1-inch-diameter white pom-pom for hat trim
Two 10-millimeter-wide white pom-poms for buttons
¼ yard of 1-inch-wide white cotton fringe for beard
Powder blush
Small artist's brush
Two 4-millimeter black beads or two black E beads
Black sewing thread
Red sewing thread
Hot-glue gun
Glue sticks
Scissors
Two 12-inch-long pieces of ⅜-inch-diameter PVC clear flexible tubing for Santa arm/leg pieces

INSTRUCTIONS

Trace the patterns, *opposite,* onto tracing paper and cut out.

Cut two body pieces from the red felt and one face from ecru felt. In addition, cut two 3-inch-diameter circles from green felt for mittens and two 3½-inch-diameter circles from black felt for boots.

Stack the body pieces on top of each other to make a double layer. Sew the center back seam using ¼ inch for a seam allowance.

Cut the body slits, then fold the cut edges to the wrong side and secure with hot glue. Turn the body right side out.

Cut a strip of the white diaper flannel to fit around the bottom of the body, including ½ inch of flannel for an overlap.

Fold the width of the strip in thirds; glue folded strip around lower edge for fur. Glue the two small pom-poms to the body at the Xs for buttons.

Make rosy cheeks on Santa's face using powder blush and a small brush. Sew eye beads in place.

Make straight-stitch eyelashes using two strands of black sewing thread. Cut a ³⁄₁₆x¼-inch oval nose from ecru felt; glue nose in place.

For beard, glue 5 inches of cotton fringe around the curved edge of the face. Glue a second strip of fringe just inside the first. Hot-glue the top of the face to the body as marked on the pattern.

Cut the white diaper flannel strip to fit around the upper body section, slightly overlapping the top of the face. Fold the strip width into thirds; glue the strip in place to make hat fur trim. Glue the large pom-pom to the tip.

For each arm/leg piece, hot glue a length of tubing to one long edge of one of the red felt rectangles. Loosely roll the tubing in the felt, making a 3½-inch-diameter arm/leg limb. Hot-glue the felt edge to secure in place.

Insert each arm/leg limb through the body slit, allowing enough room for movement.

Using running stitches, gather each green mitten circle ⅛ inch from the edge. Pull the gathers until the opening fits around the hand end of the limb. Knot the thread. Hot-glue the circle edges to the limb.

Repeat on the opposite end of each limb. Use running stitches to gather each black boot circle ⅛ inch from the edge. Pull the gathers until the opening fits around the foot end of the limb. Knot the thread. Hot-glue the circle edges in place to the limb.

Cut the white diaper flannel strip to fit around the base of each mitten and around the top of each boot, adding a ½ inch overlap to all strips. Fold the strip widths in thirds and glue in place around the mittens and boots for fur trim.

SNOWMAN LAPEL PIN AND BUTTON COVER

As shown on page 61, the lapel pin measures 1⅜x2½ inches and the button cover measures 1x2 inches.

MATERIALS
Modeling clay suitable for oven baking: white, orange, and desired colors for hat and scarf
Crafts knife
Ruler
Rolling pin or pasta press
Talcum powder
K50 Kemper rose cutter set (optional)
4-millimeter-wide round black beads
Size 0.3 black permanent ink art pen
3-millimeter-wide round black beads
Powder blush
Small artist's brush
Ultra fine iridescent glitter
Hot-glue gun
Glue sticks
1-inch-long pin back
Natural bristles from a decorative craft fan
String
Scissors
¾-inch-diameter metal button cover

INSTRUCTIONS
Knead the clay until it is pliable before attempting to roll or shape any of the pieces.

For each pin, roll a piece of orange clay into a ¼-inch-diameter ball. Shape the ball into a ⅝-inch-long carrot shape.

Using the knife and rotating the carrot shape, lightly score around the outside so shape has carrot-like ridges. Bake carrot in a 225° oven for 10 minutes. Let the shape cool.

Dust a rolling pin with talcum powder or use a pasta press on the No. 1 setting and roll white clay into a ⅛-inch-thick sheet. Cut a 1¼-inch-diameter circle for the head from the clay sheet, using a crafts knife or 1¼-inch rose cutter.

Roll out a ⅛-inch-thick sheet of clay in the color selected for the hat; cut a 1-inch-diameter circle. Cut away bottom ⅓ of circle and set the shape aside.

Put the hat on top of the white head circle, with the straight edge overlapping the circle ¼ inch.

Roll the cut-off section of the hat circle into a snake shape about 1⅛ inches long; position the shape horizontally along the bottom edge of the hat to look like a rolled brim.

Pinch off a small piece of the white clay and roll it into a ¼-inch-diameter ball. Press the ball to the top of the hat for a pom-pom. Press the orange baked carrot nose gently into the snowman face.

Position the fat end of the carrot at the center with the pointed end facing either to the left or to the right of the face, as shown in the photograph on page 61.

Press 4-millimeter-wide bead eyes in place. Draw a smile or expression using the tip of the fine-point permanent pen.

Press one 3-millimeter bead into the face at the end of the smile line, not covered by nose. Brush blush onto shape for cheeks.

Using the rolling pin or a pasta press on the No. 3 setting, prepare a ¹⁄₁₆-inch-thick sheet of clay for the scarf. Cut the piece to measure ½x3½ inches.

Tuck one end behind the lower part of the face on one side and bring the remainder across the lower face.

Tuck the scarf behind the face on the opposite side and then curl the scarf end outward. Refer to the photograph, *page 61,* for guidance. Decorate the scarf with three 3-millimeter-wide black beads.

For the button covers, follow the instructions for the lapel pin *except* use a ³⁄₁₆-inch-diameter ball to make the ½-inch-long carrot nose, a 1-inch-diameter circle for the head, ⅔ of a ¾-inch-diameter circle for the hat, a ³⁄₁₆-inch-diameter ball for a pom-pom, and 3-millimeter beads for the eyes. Cut the scarf to measure ⅜x2½ inches.

Sprinkle all the pieces with the iridescent glitter. Place on a cookie sheet and bake in a 225° oven for about 20 minutes. Allow to cool.

For the lapel pin, hot-glue the small pin back to the back of the snowman head.

Cut a 2½-inch-long bundle of bristles from the decorative craft fan. Tie the bundle in the center with the string. Hot-glue the bundle to the back of the head beneath the pin.

For each button cover, hot-glue a metal button cover to the back of the snowman head.

In a Twinkling

Every corner of your house—inside and out—will sparkle with the Christmas spirit when you create our clever lighting ideas. From a glittering lavender centerpiece to a bright and happy snowman, each idea will add a glowing warmth to your holiday home.

PHOTOGRAPHER: HOPKINS ASSOCIATES

Lavender Centerpiece

Iridescent candle rings and sparkling purple lights illuminate this elegant centerpiece. Assembled as tiny nosegays, the lighted "posies" are tucked among a lavender floral arrangement that includes violets and a flowering Christmas cactus. Instructions are on page 76.

DESIGNER: MARGARET SINDELAR
PHOTOGRAPHER: SCOTT LITTLE

Sparkling Holly Garland

Fill a gift basket with small packages, greenery, and this sparkling string of "holly" lights. It's easy to make. Just wire fabric leaves around clusters of red light "berries." Instructions and pattern are on page 76.

DESIGNER: MARGARET SINDELAR
PHOTOGRAPHER: SCOTT LITTLE

Glittering Goblets

Dip the rims of crystal-clear goblets into sparkling glitter, and you have a pretty effect. But fill the goblets to the brim with colored water and floating lit candles, and the decoration is simply glorious. Instructions are on page 76.

DESIGNER: CAROL FIELD DAHLSTROM
PHOTOGRAPHER: SCOTT LITTLE

Twinkling Jar

Here's a new ornamental for the season, and you needn't purchase a thing. Find a Mason jar or a clear antique vessel and fill it with tree lights and tiny, shiny baubles. Then let the trims flow to the foreground and top it all with ribbon for a beautiful sight! Instructions are on page 77.

DESIGNER: DONNA CHESNUT
PHOTOGRAPHER: SCOTT LITTLE

Beaded Icicles

Icicles made of pearls and golden bead caps create a heavenly sight on this starlit-and-blue-flocked garland. Like the real thing, the trims will "melt" to any length desired. (Ours are 7¾ inches long.) To add to the ethereal mood, slip angelic charms among the boughs. Instructions are on page 77.

DESIGNER: MARGARET SINDELAR
PHOTOGRAPHER: SCOTT LITTLE

Country Luminaries

Clear canning jars spread holiday cheer throughout your house when they're filled with sand, red berries, and a votive candle. Serve up several for a mantel decoration. Or, make a multitude to line your walkway and welcome all who come to call. Instructions are on page 77.

DESIGNER: DONNA CHESNUT
PHOTOGRAPHER: SCOTT LITTLE

Glimmering Icicles

The entire neighborhood will enjoy the glimmering icicles that form around your holiday home. Actually, they're white Christmas-tree lights looped and secured into the eaves. Instructions are on page 77.

DESIGNER: DAVE SMITH
PHOTOGRAPHER: SCOTT LITTLE

Happy, Lighted Snowman

This life-size snowman lights up your backyard and the holiday season with an everlasting smile. Cut from sturdy fiberboard, the self-standing figure is outlined in strings of Christmas-tree lights. A coffee-can top hat and a hand-me-down scarf make him as spiffy as can be. Instructions and patterns are on pages 77–78.

DESIGNERS: CAROL FIELD DAHLSTROM AND DONNA CHESNUT ● PHOTOGRAPHER: HOPKINS ASSOCIATES

LAVENDER CENTERPIECE

As shown on page 70.

MATERIALS

35-light strand of lavender miniature globe lights
Seven 3½-inch-diameter glass candle rings
White or green floral tape
Twenty-one 2-inch-long green satin artificial leaves
4 yards of 2-inch-wide sheer white-and-gold wire-edged ribbon
Fine gauge white cotton-wrapped floral wire
Christmas cactus; lavender cellophane
Silver floral foil; large silver tray
Five small pots of lavender violets
Evergreens; ivy

INSTRUCTIONS

For each nosegay of "violets," group five globe lights together in your hand and push bulbs through center of one candle ring. Using floral tape, wrap wires together below candle ring. Wire three artificial leaves to wrapped wires just below candle ring; wrap with additional tape if necessary to secure in place. Tie 16 inches of ribbon into a bow; wire bow at base of leaves. Cover tape with silver foil. Repeat to make seven nosegays.

Wrap pot of Christmas cactus in cellophane and foil; place pot on tray. Arrange nosegay lights, evergreens, potted African violets, and the ivy around the Christmas cactus as desired.

SPARKLING HOLLY GARLAND

SPARKLING HOLLY GARLAND

As shown on page 70.

MATERIALS

Tracing paper
Paper-backed iron-on adhesive
¼ yard *each* of two different Christmas cotton prints
Fine- and medium-gauge cotton-wrapped floral wire
Gold glitter paint
Small round artist's brush
35-light strand of red miniature globe lights
Green floral tape; evergreen sprigs
Large red basket with handle
Two gold Christmas bell ornaments
Large red, green, and gold wire-edged ribbon bow

INSTRUCTIONS

Trace the holly leaf pattern, *below left,* onto tracing paper; cut out. Draw around the pattern on the paper side of the paper-backed adhesive 30 times.

Following the manufacturer's instructions, fuse leaves to wrong side of one fabric. Cut out leaves and remove paper backing.

For each leaf, position a 4-inch-long piece of fine-gauge wire down center line of each leaf on wrong side, allowing excess wire to extend beyond bottom of leaf. Fuse leaf to fabric, sandwiching wire between layers; cut out fused leaf. Repeat for all leaves. Paint leaf veins using gold glitter paint and a round brush.

Group three, four, or five lights together in your hand; wrap wires together below bulbs using floral tape. Wire two or three leaves to light cluster below bulbs and wrap with additional floral tape to secure in place. Repeat this process until all of lights are clustered.

Wire evergreens to rim of basket using medium-gauge wire. Wire bells to bow. Wire bow and several holly light clusters to the basket handle. Wire the remainder of the lights around the rim of the basket, hiding wire ends in greenery. Fill basket as desired.

GLITTERING GOBLETS

As shown on page 71.

MATERIALS

Clear crystal goblets
White tacky glue
Small bowl
Golden glitter
Food coloring
Floating candles

INSTRUCTIONS

Wash and dry goblets. Carefully cover rim of each goblet with white tacky glue. Fill a small bowl or dish with golden glitter. Press goblet rims into glitter. Let dry.

Carefully fill goblets with colored water; float a candle in each.

TWINKLING JAR

As shown on page 71.

MATERIALS

Glass ornaments in various shapes
   and sizes to fit inside jar
Short strand of clear Christmas lights
Pieces of real or artificial greenery
Large wide-mouth jar
1 yard of 1-inch-wide gold ribbon

INSTRUCTIONS

Beginning with the end of the
strand of lights opposite the plug,
tuck lights, ornaments, and greenery
randomly into jar. Allow plug end of
strand of lights to remain outside jar
for use with an extension cord.

Pile additional ornaments on top.
Tie gold ribbon around mouth of jar.

Add more lights, ornaments, and
greenery around the base to create a
centerpiece, if desired.

BEADED ICICLES

*As shown on page 72, each orna-
ment is 7¾ inches long. For longer
or shorter icicles, vary the length of
the metallic thread and the number
of bead caps and pearl beads.*

MATERIALS

for each ornament
24 inches of gold metallic thread
One 4-millimeter pearl bead
Seven 12-millimeter pearl beads
Five 8-millimeter pearl beads
Four 6-millimeter pearl beads
Three 14-millimeter gold bead caps
One 10-millimeter gold bead cap
One 2-inch-long gold bolo tip
Fine beading needle

INSTRUCTIONS

Thread needle with the 24-inch
length of gold metallic thread.

Allow 6½ inches for a tail at the
beginning, then thread pearl beads
and gold bead caps in the following
order: One 4-millimeter pearl bead,
one 14-millimeter gold bead cap
with the cup side up, seven 12-mil-
limeter pearl beads, one 14-millime-
ter gold bead cap with the cup side

down, one 10-millimeter gold bead
cap with the cup side up, five 8-mil-
limeter pearl beads, three 6-millime-
ter pearl beads, one 14-millimeter
gold bead cap with the cup side up,
and the last 6-millimeter pearl bead.

Thread needle through holes in the
top of the bolo tip and back through
all pieces, in reverse.

Knot the thread at the top of the
first pearl bead. Then knot ends of
the thread to make a hanging loop.

Squeeze the bottom bead cap over
the bottom pearl and top of bolo tip.

Vary the patterns of pearl beads
and bead caps as desired to make
longer or shorter icicles.

COUNTRY LUMINARIES

As shown on page 73.

MATERIALS

Quart- or pint-size Mason jars; sand
Sugar scoop or gardener's hand trowel
Candle in glass votive cups, one for
   each jar
Real or artificial evergreen sprigs and
   holly berries
Red-and-green plaid ribbon
Red and green tinsel

INSTRUCTIONS

For each luminary, fill bottom
¼ to ⅓ of jar with sand. Firmly press
a candle down into sand. Drop small
bits of greenery or berries into the
jar. Tie ribbon around top of jar and
tuck tinsel around bow.

GLIMMERING ICICLES

As shown on page 74.

MATERIALS

Strands of clear miniature outdoor lights
1-inch-wide PVC pipe in desired length
Plastic cable ties (available at home
   centers)

INSTRUCTIONS

Cut PVC pipe into desired
lengths to fit into eaves spouts.
Using cable ties, secure lights to
pipe looping lights down and up to

pipe at random lengths. Using ties,
attach lights together to give the
appearance of one icicle per loop
(see diagram *below.*) Place pipe with
lights attached into eaves spouts.

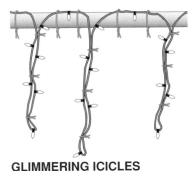

GLIMMERING ICICLES

HAPPY, LIGHTED SNOWMAN

*As shown on page 75, snowman
without hat measures 24x48 inches.*

MATERIALS

4x8-foot piece of ¾-inch particleboard
Tape measure; pencil; jigsaw
12-inch piece of 1-inch-diameter dowel
5-inch piece of ½-inch-diameter dowel
Drill; ½- and 1-inch drill bits
Sharp knife
39-ounce coffee can (6¾ inches tall
   with a 7⅛-inch diameter)
White, black, and orange spray paints
Three white Christmas light strings
Grapevine branches; scarf
Artificial greens and berry stems
Construction adhesive; caulk gun

INSTRUCTIONS

For snowman front/back, measure 12½ inches from edge on one
8-foot side of board; lightly draw a
line the entire length of the particleboard, referring to the diagram,
page 78. Beginning at the 4-foot
side (the bottom edge) of the board,
measure along the marked line at
10½-, 29½-, and 42-inch intervals,
and mark each with a dot.

Beginning at bottom of board
and using the 10½-inch mark as
center point, draw a 24-inch-diame-
ter circle. Draw an 18- and 12-inch
circle in same manner using dots as
center of the circles. *Note:* The
circles will overlap.

For slot-cutting lines, measure and mark a dot along the center line 24 inches from the bottom of the board. Draw a parallel line 3/8 inch from the center line on each side of line to create a 3/4-inch-wide slot.

For snowman sides, measure 34 inches from opposite 8-foot edge of particleboard and draw another center line the full length of particleboard. Measure and draw 24-inch and 18-inch-diameter circles in same manner as directed on page 77 for snowman shape. Measure and mark cutting lines for slot as directed before.

Draw two 2½-inch-diameter eyes, three 3½-inch-diameter buttons, and one 10-inch-diameter hat brim circle in an open area of particleboard. Cut out all of the pieces, including slots.

For nose, drill a 1-inch-diameter hole 3/4-inch-deep along center line of snowman front/back 4½ inches from top of the head. For buttons, mark and cut a 3/4-inch strip from the center of each of the 3½-inch-diameter button circles. Set aside the half-circle shapes. Drill a ½-inch-diameter hole 1-inch-deep into top center of snowman's head and in center of hat brim. Drill a ½-inch-diameter hole in each side of snowman front/back 6 inches from neck for inserting arms.

For light sockets, measure and drill 3/8-inch holes every 2 inches around perimeter of snowman front/back and side pieces. Drill a ½-inch hole in throat to pass light string through to the front. For the mouth, cut seven 3/8-inch-thick discs from 1-inch-diameter dowel.

For nose, use a sharp knife to shave wood from one end of dowel until it resembles a carrot. Center coffee-can container on hat brim; adhere in place using construction adhesive. Push dowel into hat brim, adhering in place with construction adhesive. Paint snowman body

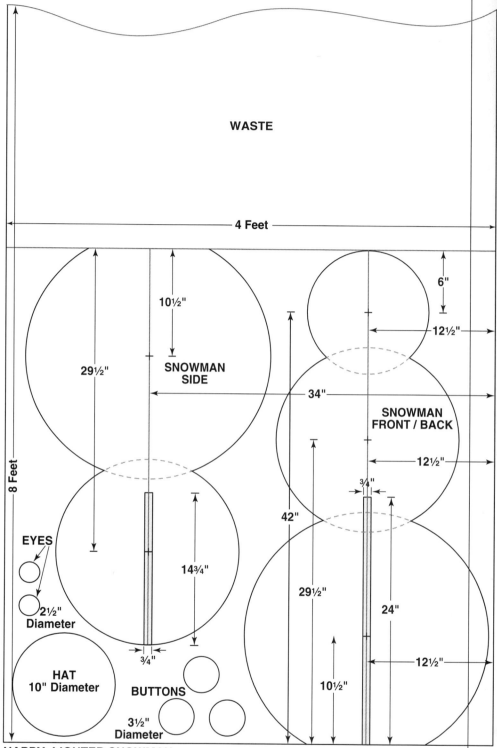

HAPPY, LIGHTED SNOWMAN

pieces white; eyes, buttons, hat brim, mouth pieces, and coffee-can black; and nose orange. Assemble snowman front/back and snowman side pieces together, matching slots and slipping pieces together. Cement eyes, nose, mouth, both button circles, and bottom button half-circles in place with adhesive.

Beginning at bottom of snowman front/back, insert lights into drilled openings around body. Repeat for snowman side, passing light string through the opening in neck to front.

Insert dowel on hat into the opening at the top of head. Insert grapevine arms into armholes; tie scarf around snowman's neck.

Christmas Past

*Come share the memories of a Christmas long ago.
The centerpiece of the occasion is the glorious evergreen tree
trimmed with shiny tinsel, magical beaded stars, and sweet
paper angels. Sugar candy, spicy gingerbread treats, and
a perfect steamed pudding complete this glorious
and memorable holiday celebration.*

PHOTOGRAPHER: HOPKINS ASSOCIATES

Victorian Elegance

A charming Christmas of long ago is re-created with our collection of ornaments inspired by exquisite antique trims. Sparkling tinsel, subtle colors, and unlimited embellishments so typical of Victorian times, fill our naturally shaped evergreen tree. Turn the page for some fascinating history and helps for re-creating this beautiful vision of days gone by.

DESIGNERS: ANTIQUE ADAPTATIONS BY MARGARET SINDELAR,
CAROL DAHLSTROM, AND ARDITH FIELD
PHOTOGRAPHER: HOPKINS ASSOCIATES

The Tree of Christmas Past

For decades, the evergreen tree has been the centerpiece of Christmas decorating. In Victorian times, the tree was the home for all things sparkling and glorious. Here we share some fascinating history about the Christmas-tree tradition that may inspire you to create romantic trims of your own. Instructions, patterns, and special tips for re-creating the elegant antique ornaments featured on pages 82–84, begin on page 89.

PHOTOGRAPHER: HOPKINS ASSOCIATES

It's Christmas morning in a Victorian home. The family gathers outside the closed parlor door while Father sets the candles alight. When the tree is aglow, he throws open the parlor door and ushers in the family. It's a magical moment—the children's first sight of the glorious, glittering Christmas tree.

Bright, shining eyes behold snow fairies that twirl slowly and tiny tapers that flicker and glow. Gilded apples and beaded gold stars catch the candlelight, and silver tinsel and golden Christmas balls twinkle. The tree is massed with ornaments and gifts. Paper cornucopias are filled with candy and nuts. Sachets and needle cases for Mother are suspended from ribbons. Tin soldiers and small dolls with china heads are perched on the branches, ready for little fingers to pluck. Father discovers a

This antique star-in-a-circle ornament was probably made in Czechoslovakia about 1900. It is a good example of a glass-bead ornament.

This rare photo of a Victorian Christmas tree and the toys that surround it, is valuable research for those Christmas-lovers interested in Christmases past. The photo was taken about 1880 and can be seen at the Toy and Miniature Museum in Kansas City, Missouri.

PHOTOGRAPH: COURTESY OF THE JOSEPH B. HALL FAMILY

Paper ornaments were embellished with favorite "scrap" pictures and dusted with glitter creating a heavenly effect. This ornament was probably made about 1875.

comb, a brush, and a miniature English flag hidden among the boughs. Larger, heavier gifts are artfully arranged, unwrapped, at the base of the tree.

The evergreen centerpiece, the Christmas tree, gained popularity in England in the 1840s. Legend credits Prince Albert, husband of Queen Victoria, with bringing the Christmas tree to England from his native Germany. Actually, the English royal family had been "dressing" Christmas trees for at least 50 years prior. However, historians believe it was Albert that

Crepe paper was often used to create a background of color for the scrap image. This one features an angel with tinsel glued over the paper and was probably made about 1880.

This lavish tree was decorated in the Victorian style with antique ornaments from the collection of Christopher Filley and Rich Hoffman and displayed in the Toy and Miniature Museum in Kansas City, Missouri. Over 600 ornaments were individually hung to create the elegant effect.

popularized the custom. He often presented decorated trees to schools and army barracks. In 1848, the *Illustrated London News* published a full-page drawing depicting Prince Albert's tree at Windsor Castle. After that, the Christmas-tree tradition was enthusiastically adopted by the English middle class, and it spread throughout the country.

Prince Albert's tree, prepared for the royal children, was customarily an untrimmed Douglas fir, about 8 feet tall with six tiers of branches. Dozens of candles in metal holders were fastened on each branch. Sweet treats hung from the branches. Small baskets and trays were filled with candies; fancy cakes and gingerbread were suspended by colorful ribbons. A small angel or a tinseled

Hearts were a favorite motif of the Victorians no matter what the season. This heart was made with tinsel and glass balls.

star perched atop the tree.

As the Christmas-tree tradition developed, edible decorations were augmented by handmade ornaments and gifts. Victorians loved color and glitter, lace and ribbons, fairy figures and flowers. Those favored things—and more—were fastened to the boughs of the Christmas tree. Stars, hearts, harps, open on a branch or suspended with a fine wire. Children's handicrafts, too, adorned the tree: Paper chains and paper dolls, strings of red berries, popcorn balls, and bouquets of paper roses.

Scrap pictures were another favorite tree ornament. These romantic drawings of angels, cherubs, nativity scenes, Santas, and elegant ladies were printed on heavy paper in both England and Germany. Printing process allowed 19 to 20 colors, so pictures were beautifully detailed and colorful. After printing, they were embossed to create a feeling of dimension. Little girls used the pictures as paper dolls.

Victorian women collected them, preserving the pictures in scrapbooks, thus earning the name scrap pictures. Women often decorated the scrap pictures before they hung them on the Christmas tree. Santa's beard or an angel's cloud, for example, might be puffed with cotton. A picture of an elegant lady might be embellished with ribbon, lace, and feathers.

By the 1890s, German printers were producing special scrap Christmas ornaments, embellished by tinsel, spun glass, or angel's hair. From 1870 to 1890, store-bought ornaments, imported from Germany, gained commercial success in both England and America. They were made of cardboard, wax, tin, tinsel, and glass.

Multifaceted stars, crosses, and butterflies were molded of tin. Figurines of the Holy Child, children, and animals were molded from wax. Glassblowers, also working with molds, created colorful balls, pine cones, acorns, apples, pears, birds with spun-glass tail feathers, houses, and churches.

Each Christmas brought new and more dazzling ornaments to the Victorian-era Christmas tree.

In the 1890s, glass-bead ornaments and ropes were imported from Czechoslovakia. The ornament makers strung their colored beads on thin wire formed in geometric shapes. As ornaments became more plentiful, varied, and intricate, the Victorian Christmas tree became even more elaborate.

To make space for the bounty, the tree trimmers dressed the tree in three vertical layers, from the inside out. The first layer of ornaments was suspended near the trunk. Then, tree trimmers moved outward, hanging ornaments from the center of branches. The gifts and remaining ornaments were attached to the outer tips of the branches. Some were suspended from fine filaments and ribbons and others were set gently on top of the branches. This final layer of decorations included candles, glass-bead ropes, and tinsel garlands.

Glorious trees that filled homes of Christmas past took center stage, as do trimmed evergreens that we lovingly create today.

To re-create the seven ornaments we have featured, turn to page 89.

This antique tree topper is made from crepe paper and tinsel and measures 11x11 inches. A coiled wire at the star base is used as the method of securing it to the tree.

and crescents were cut from bright or shiny paper or fashioned from tinsel. Walnuts, acorns, and apples were gilded or painted silver. Lace bags were stuffed with colorful candies. Lace gloves were filled with potpourri. Fans crafted of colored paper were trimmed with lace, ribbons, and bows, then propped

This spun glass ornament was probably made about 1900, and features a delicate scrap angel in the center of the circle.

This Victorian-era ornament is typical of ones created in the late 1800s. Tinsel rope and glass balls were combined in various shapes and combinations.

Satin Ribbon Stocking

Filled to the brim with vintage treasures, our holiday stocking is a cache of satin ribbons. The ribbons are woven and treated as a single layer of fabric, stitched into an elegant stocking, and then trimmed with piping.
Instructions are on page 95.

DESIGNER: DIANNE SHEPHERD
PHOTOGRAPHER: HOPKINS ASSOCIATES

Gingerbread Noah's Ark

Children of all ages will gather around to hear the story of Noah and the Ark—and to share the tastes and smells of the spicy gingerbread. The ark is constructed with flat pieces of gingerbread and then piped with colorful frosting. Dozens of pairs of animals can be made two by two using favorite animal cookie cutters. Instructions and patterns start on page 96.

DESIGNER: CAROL FIELD DAHLSTROM ● PHOTOGRAPHER: HOPKINS ASSOCIATES

Sweet Treats

Candy, as sweet as can be, has always been a delicious part of Christmastime. Our candy collection features easy Chocolate-Almond Truffles, Grandma's Fudge, and two flavors of heavenly divinity. Recipes and easy step-by-step tips start on page 98.

PHOTOGRAPHER: SCOTT LITTLE

Victorian Steamed Pudding

A sweet orange-juice flavored frosting delicately covers our favorite steamed pudding. A traditional Christmas dessert for generations, the pudding is steamed in a slow cooker and then unmolded and presented on an antique cake plate. The recipe is on page 100.

PHOTOGRAPHER: SCOTT LITTLE

BEADED STAR ORNAMENT

Antique Ornament

Reproduction Ornament

BEADED STAR ORNAMENT

As shown on pages 80–81 and above, ornament is 3½ inches in diameter. Note: *Wired beads are available in a bendable wire strand. They're packaged on spools and sold by the yard at craft stores.*

MATERIALS
16 inches of silver wired bead strand
12 inches of gold wired bead strand
Fine-gauge craft wire
Assorted small gold beads
Six colored bugle beads
One 5-millimeter-diameter red bead

BEADED STAR ORNAMENT

INSTRUCTIONS
Bend the silver bead strand into a star shape following the star outline pattern *below.* Cut away the excess bead strand and wire the ends together at the top.

Bend the gold bead strand to form a circle around the star with points of star touching the inside of the circle. Wire the top star point to the circle. Wire each bottom point to the circle, leaving 4-inch-long wire tails.

String two bugle beads and then seven to 10 small gold beads in the desired pattern onto each wire. Bring the wires together and thread a red bead over both wires.

Separate the wires once again; string the remaining gold and colored beads in the established pattern on each wire until only ½ inch of unbeaded wire remains. Bend the wire ends up and poke them back through the second bead from the bottom to secure in place.

Attach thread or wire at the top for a hanging loop.

SCALLOP OVAL WITH SUNBURST

As shown on pages 80–81 and 91, ornament measures 5³⁄4x7 inches.

MATERIALS
Tracing paper
10x16-inch piece of lightweight posterboard
Scissors with scalloped blades made for decorative paper edging
Spray adhesive
Spray paint: white, hot pink, and gold
Non-tarnishing glitter
Crafts glue
Victorian scrap angel or reproduction angel card measuring approximately 4½x4½ inches
1x1-inch square of foamcore
8 inches of gold metallic thread
Bright blue dimensional fabric paint

INSTRUCTIONS
Trace patterns, *page 90,* onto tracing paper and cut out. Draw around patterns onto posterboard to make two ovals, two sunbursts, and one small star. Cut out posterboard pieces. Cut around edge of each oval using the scallop blade scissors. Glue ovals back to back using spray adhesive. Glue sunbursts back to back in the same manner.

Spray center of oval and upper part of sunburst white. Spray bottom third of oval, points of sunburst, and small star hot pink. Lightly spray top third of oval, center of sunburst, and small star with gold paint. While paint is wet, sprinkle pieces generously with non-tarnishing glitter. Allow to dry.

Glue angel to oval with most of the angel showing above the dotted

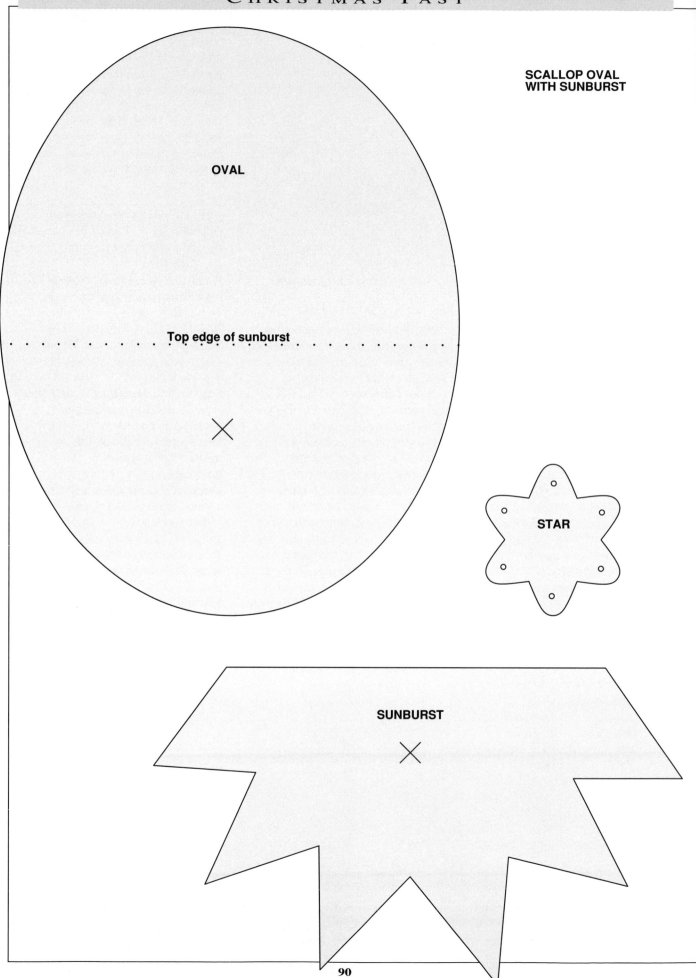

**SCALLOP OVAL
WITH SUNBURST**

OVAL

Top edge of sunburst

STAR

SUNBURST

SCALLOP OVAL WITH SUNBURST

Antique Ornament

Reproduction Ornament

line indicating top edge of sunburst. Glue foamcore to X on oval. Glue sunburst atop the foamcore piece, matching the top edge to the dotted line on oval. Glue small star to X on sunburst. Add blue paint dots to star.

Pierce hole in the top of the ornament and tie with gold thread for a hanging loop.

ANGEL ON CREPE PAPER CIRCLE

As shown on pages 80–81 and below, ornament measures about 4x4½ inches.

MATERIALS
Two 4-inch-diameter lightweight posterboard circles
Spray adhesive
3 yards of red crepe paper streamer
Clear acrylic spray varnish
Tape
Gold spray paint
12 inches of gold tinsel garland
Brown liquid shoe polish
24-gauge craft wire
Victorian scrap angel or reproduction angel card measuring about 3½x4 inches
12 inches of gold metallic thread

INSTRUCTIONS
Glue posterboard circles back to back using spray adhesive. Cut crepe paper streamer in half lengthwise. Tape one end of one crepe paper

strip to one side of circle at center. Wrap streamer around circle, lapping edges in spiral fashion until the posterboard circle is covered. While wrapping, stretch crepe paper so it is snug but does not bend the circle. Tape end of crepe paper at center when finished.

Spray entire circle with varnish; allow to dry. Next, spray lightly with gold paint.

Trim fringe on tinsel garland to measure ½ inch. Rub brown shoe polish over garland for an antique look; let dry. Cut garland length in half. Poke two tiny holes in center of circle. Hold garland lengths together in the center; wire center to circle front. Arrange garland lengths; glue angel card to circle atop the garland.

Poke a small hole in the top of the ornament. Tie gold thread through the hole for a hanging loop.

TINSEL HEART

As shown on pages 80–81 and 92, heart measures 6x7 inches.

MATERIALS
Tracing paper
Pen
8x10-inch piece of corrugated cardboard
Straight pins
Narrow-looped silver tinsel garland
Craft wire
One 1-inch-diameter gold Christmas ball ornament
Three 1-inch-diameter green Christmas ball ornaments
Silver tinsel
Gold spray paint
8 inches of silver metallic thread

INSTRUCTIONS
Trace pattern, *page 92,* onto tracing paper. Lay tracing atop the cardboard. Trace firmly over pattern lines using the pen, leaving the imprint of the pattern in the cardboard. Push pins into the cardboard every inch along the imprint and at the turning or crossing points.

Wind wire tightly around the silver tinsel garland in a spiral fashion so the garland will hold its shape when it is bent. Following the arrows shown on the pattern, *page 92,* begin at A and bend the wired garland around pins to B, forming the heart shape. Secure ends by twisting them around the wired-garland of the heart shape.

ANGEL ON CREPE PAPER CIRCLE

Antique Ornament

Reproduction Ornament

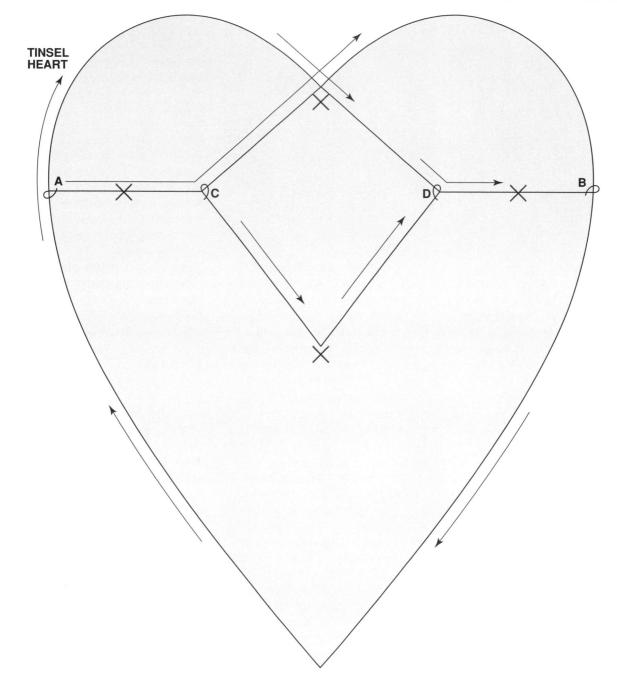

TINSEL HEART

TINSEL
HEART

A ✕ C D ✕ B

TINSEL HEART

Antique Ornament

Reproduction Ornament

In the same manner, add wired garland for the heart center from C to D and then from E to F, twisting and securing garland to the heart shape as needed.

Secure center at top X with wire. Then wire a gold ball to the heart at the red X at the top of the center diamond. Wire a green ball to each remaining red X.

Tie strands of tinsel to the bottom point of the heart. Spray entire ornament with gold paint to give it the look of an antique.

Antique Ornament

Reproduction Ornament

VICTORIAN STAR TREE TOPPER

As shown on pages 80–81 and above, star measures 11 inches across.

MATERIALS

Graph paper
Two 10½x14-inch pieces of clear 10-count plastic canvas
Eight 12-inch-long silver tinsel stems
Fine-gauge craft wire
15 feet of silver tinsel garland
6x6-inch piece of posterboard
6x12-inch piece of gold floral foil
Red spray paint

INSTRUCTIONS

Enlarge star pattern, *below,* onto graph paper and cut out.

Using the star pattern, cut two stars from the 10-count clear plastic canvas. Whipstitch the stars together around the outer edge using the 12-inch-long silver tinsel stems and leaving the star open between the bottom two points.

Using pieces of wire, attach tinsel garland to star front and back, reserving 24 inches of tinsel garland for center star. First wire garland around perimeter of the star, then fill in center. Set the star aside.

Cut a 5-inch-diameter scalloped circle from the posterboard, cutting each scallop to span approximately 1½ inches. Clip 1 inch toward the center of the circle between each scallop.

Cover the front and back of the scalloped posterboard piece with gold foil, cutting slits to match those on the posterboard shape. Using fingers, bend and curve gold foil scallops toward the front of the shape. Spray both sides of shape with red paint; allow to dry.

Trim the fringe on the 24-inch-long piece of tinsel garland to ½ inch. Loop tinsel into a five-point star; wire together at center to hold shape. Punch two small holes in center of scalloped circle and wire small tinsel star to the center. Wire scalloped circle to center front of large star. Trim tinsel at star points. Lightly spray star with gold paint.

TRUMPETING CHERUB ON CIRCLE

As shown on pages 80–81 and page 94, ornament measures approximately 5 inches in diameter.

MATERIALS

Two 4-inch-diameter posterboard circles
Spray adhesive; crafts glue
Silver tinsel garland; white spray paint
1x1-inch square of foamcore
Victorian scrap angel or reproduction angel card, measuring approximately 3½ inches wide
12 inches of silver metallic thread

INSTRUCTIONS

Glue the two posterboard circles back to back using spray adhesive. Next, glue silver tinsel garland around the front of the posterboard circle, overlapping the edge of the circle approximately ½ inch. Lightly spray tinsel with white paint.

Glue the square of foamcore to the center front of the circle and glue scrap angel to the foamcore.

Poke a hole in the top of the ornament. Tie a silver cord through the hole for a hanging loop.

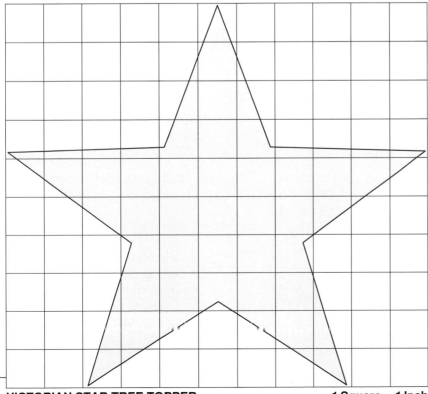

VICTORIAN STAR TREE TOPPER   **1 Square = 1 Inch**

TRUMPETING CHERUB ON CIRCLE

Antique Ornament

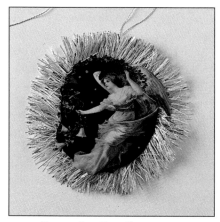

Reproduction Ornament

DIAMOND TINSEL ORNAMENT

As shown on pages 80–81 and above right, ornament measures about 5½x5½ inches.

MATERIALS

Four 12-inch-long silver tinsel pipe cleaner stems
2 feet of silver tinsel garland
24-gauge craft wire
Four 1-inch-diameter silver Christmas ball ornaments
Gold spray paint
Red spray paint
6 inches of silver metallic thread

INSTRUCTIONS

Bend silver tinsel pipe cleaner stems, referring to the pattern, *below,* into a 4x4-inch square. Add the individual cross pieces next, twisting stems around each other, as necessary, to secure in place.

Trim tinsel fringe on garland to measure ½- to ¾-inch long. Wrap garland around tinsel frame. Secure with wire.

Use wire to attach a silver ball to the red Xs at the top and center of the pattern, referring to the photograph, *below right,* for placement. Then lightly spray the entire ornament with gold paint to give it the look of an antique.

To "antique" the red balls, dip the remaining silver balls into water and spray with red paint. Allow to dry. Wire balls to the ornament at red Xs at sides.

Tie a silver thread to the top for a hanging loop.

DIAMOND TINSEL ORNAMENT

Antique Ornament

Reproduction Ornament

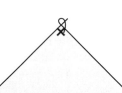

DIAMOND TINSEL ORNAMENT

SATIN RIBBON STOCKING

As shown on page 85, stocking measures 17 inches long.

MATERIALS
Graph paper
½ yard of sheer black lightweight fusible interfacing
½ yard of small burgundy-and-green plaid
¾ yard of burgundy satin
Size 12 bias tape maker for a ½ inch finished width
Grid paper for ribbon pin-weaving
16x21-inch piece of cardboard
Quilting pins
12 yards of ¼-inch-wide burgundy satin ribbon
1⅞ yards of ⅛-inch-wide mauve ribbon
1⅞ yards of ½-inch-wide burgundy upholstery gimp
1⅞ yards of ¼-inch-wide mauve satin picot ribbon
1⅞ yards of ½-inch-wide mauve upholstery gimp
Nylon sewing thread
⅝ yard of burgundy velveteen
Burgundy sewing thread
½ yard of ½-inch-diameter burgundy upholstery cording

INSTRUCTIONS
Enlarge stocking pattern, *above right,* onto graph paper. Mark right side of stocking "front;" cut out the pattern piece. With the wrong side of the pattern facing the fusible side of the interfacing, cut the interfacing ½ inch larger than the pattern all around. Cut a 6x19-inch rectangle of interfacing for the cuff.

Cut plaid fabric into 1-inch-wide strips, cutting with the straight grain. Cut 1-inch-wide strips of burgundy satin, cutting from selvage to selvage. Use bias tape maker to fold and press the long cut edges to wrong side, creating ½-inch-wide strips for weaving.

Lay grid paper on top of cardboard. Position the interfacing stocking, fusible side up, on the grid paper. Pin the stocking to the board at the edge of the toe, heel, and the top two corners.

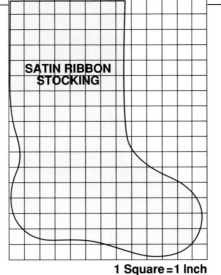

1 Square = 1 Inch

To lay warp (lengthwise ribbons), pin ¼-inch-wide burgundy ribbon on far left vertical grid line, starting at top left edge of interfacing stocking. Smooth ribbon down interfacing stocking; pin in place at bottom. Cut ribbon just beyond pin. Repeat with ⅛-inch-wide mauve ribbon on next vertical grid line. Continue across the interfacing using burgundy gimp, ¼-inch mauve picot ribbon, ¼-inch burgundy ribbon, mauve gimp, and ¼-inch burgundy ribbon. Repeat sequence across interfacing stocking until covered. Pins must be on the edge of the interfacing, on vertical grid line, and follow the contour of the pattern as shown on the pinning diagram, *above right.*

Weave plaid fabric strips over and under warp, working from left to right and from top to bottom. Extend strips at sides to cover entire fusible surface. Keep strips close together and level, using grid lines as guides.

With pins still in board, press entire piece according to manufacturer's instructions for interfacing. Remove pins, turn weaving over, and press from back.

Repeat pinning and weaving for cuff, using ¼-inch-wide burgundy ribbon for warp and weaving with burgundy satin fabric strips.

Stitch in a random wavy pattern over stocking using nylon thread in the top of the machine and burgundy thread in the bobbin. For cuff, stitch across weaving "in the ditch" between fabric strips. Lay paper stocking pattern over woven stocking

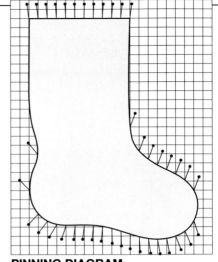

PINNING DIAGRAM

and cut out. Cut the cuff 12 strips high by 18 inches wide. Straight-stitch around the woven pieces close to the edge.

Cut stocking back from burgundy velveteen. Cut two more stockings (reversing one) from burgundy satin for the lining. Cut cuff lining from satin using the woven cuff for the pattern. Cut a 2¼x7-inch hanging loop from burgundy satin.

Unless otherwise indicated, sew fabric shapes together with right sides facing, using ½-inch seams.

Sew stocking front to back leaving the top edge open; trim seam and clip curves. Repeat for lining. Turn stocking right side out and press. Slip lining inside stocking with wrong sides facing. Set aside.

Using zipper foot, stitch cording to the right side of one long edge of woven cuff. With right sides facing, place cuff lining atop woven cuff and sew along cording seam line.

Open piece out, then fold it crosswise, with right sides facing and matching short sides. Sew sides together, forming a tube. Turn cuff right side out, then fold lining to inside. Baste raw edges together.

Fold hanging loop strip in half lengthwise with right sides facing; sew long edges together. Turn and press. Fold strip in half crosswise and pin to back seam on wrong side of stocking, matching raw edges. Slip cuff into stocking with right side of cuff facing stocking lining. Sew cuff to stocking, matching raw edges; turn cuff to outside.

GINGERBREAD RECIPE

Pictured on page 86. For Noah's ark and animals, make this recipe twice; don't double it.

INGREDIENTS
- ½ cup butter or margarine, softened
- ½ cup shortening
- 1 cup sugar
- 1½ teaspoons ground ginger
- 1½ teaspoons ground allspice
- 1 teaspoon baking soda
- ½ teaspoon salt
- 1 egg
- ½ cup molasses
- 2 tablespoons lemon juice
- 3 cups all-purpose flour
- 1 cup whole wheat flour

METHOD

In a large mixing bowl, beat butter or margarine and shortening with an electric mixer on medium to high speed for 30 seconds. Add sugar, ginger, allspice, soda, and salt and beat till combined. Add egg, molasses, and lemon juice and beat till combined. Beat in as much of the all-purpose flour as you can with the mixer. Stir in any remaining all-purpose flour and the whole wheat flour with a wooden spoon. Divide dough in half; wrap halves in clear plastic wrap. Chill for 3 hours or till firm enough to roll out.

ROYAL ICING

Pictured on page 86. For Noah's ark and animals, make this recipe twice; don't double it.

INGREDIENTS
- 3 tablespoons meringue powder
- ⅓ cup warm water
- 1 16-ounce package powdered sugar, sifted (4½ cups)
- 1 teaspoon vanilla
- ½ teaspoon cream of tartar
- Paste food coloring

METHOD

In a small mixing bowl, combine meringue powder, water, powdered sugar, vanilla, and cream of tartar. Beat with an electric mixer on low speed till combined, then on high speed for 7 to 10 minutes or till very stiff. Use at once.

Divide icing and tint with paste food coloring. When not using icing, keep it covered with clear plastic wrap to prevent it from drying out. Makes 3 cups.

GINGERBREAD NOAH'S ARK AND ANIMALS

As shown on cover and page 86, ark measures 4x12x8 inches.

MATERIALS
Tracing paper
Clear adhesive plastic (optional)
Gingerbread recipe, *left*
Royal Icing recipe, *below left*
2 to 2½-inch Animal Cookie Cutters
  (we used Wilton brand cutters)
Pastry bags, couplers, and tips
  (we used small round and star tips)
Candy-coated fruit-flavored pieces
  (we used Skittles)
Candy canes
Striped round peppermint candies
  (we used Starlight Mints)
Waxed paper or aluminum foil

INSTRUCTIONS

To make ark, enlarge patterns, *opposite,* onto tracing paper. If desired, cover both sides of pattern pieces with clear adhesive plastic. This will protect patterns from grease so they can be used again.

Using a floured rolling pin, roll out cookie dough ⅛- to ¼-inch thick on the back of an ungreased 15x10x1-inch baking pan. Place patterns 1 inch apart on dough; cut around patterns with a sharp knife. Remove excess dough.

Bake pieces in a 375° oven for 10 to 12 minutes or till edges are lightly browned. While cookie pieces are still very warm, place patterns on cookies and trim excess cookie as necessary. For easier assembly, cookies should be cut as exact as possible. Return cookies to oven for 2 to 3 minutes or till firm in center. Cool cookies on baking pan for about 2 minutes. Loosen from baking pan with a spatula. When nearly cool, transfer to a wire rack to cool completely. Repeat till all pattern pieces have been baked.

To make animal cookies, roll out dough ⅛- to ¼-inch thick on a lightly floured surface. Use animal cutters to cut out cookies. To make stands for cookies, cut out triangles from some of the rolled dough using a sharp knife. Triangles should be about 2 inches tall.

Place shapes 1 inch apart on a lightly greased baking sheet. Bake in a 375° oven for 8 to 9 minutes or till edges are lightly browned. Remove to a wire rack to cool.

To decorate ark and animals, fit pastry bags with couplers and tips. Fill with Royal Icing. Decorate shapes as desired. Attach fruit-flavored candy pieces while icing is still wet. Candy canes and peppermint candies are added after assembly. Let pieces dry for several hours or overnight before assembling. If tips dry shut during decorating, wipe with a damp cloth. Prepared Royal Icing may be held overnight in refrigerator; beat with an electric mixer again till very stiff.

To assemble ark, use glass measuring cups or coffee mugs to hold pieces in place. Position ark base on a piece of waxed paper or foil. Pipe icing on one long edge. Immediately attach one of the ark sides. Hold in place with measuring cups or mugs. Meanwhile, attach front and back of ark cabin to the base, then attach other side of ark to ark base, piping more icing where pieces join. When these pieces are set (about 20 minutes) continue with ends of ark, cabin sides, and cabin roof. (Cabin roof may take longer to set.) Attach candy canes and peppermint candies as a finishing touch to ark.

Attach cookies to their triangle stands, using more icing. Let dry completely, cookie face down, before standing cookies upright.

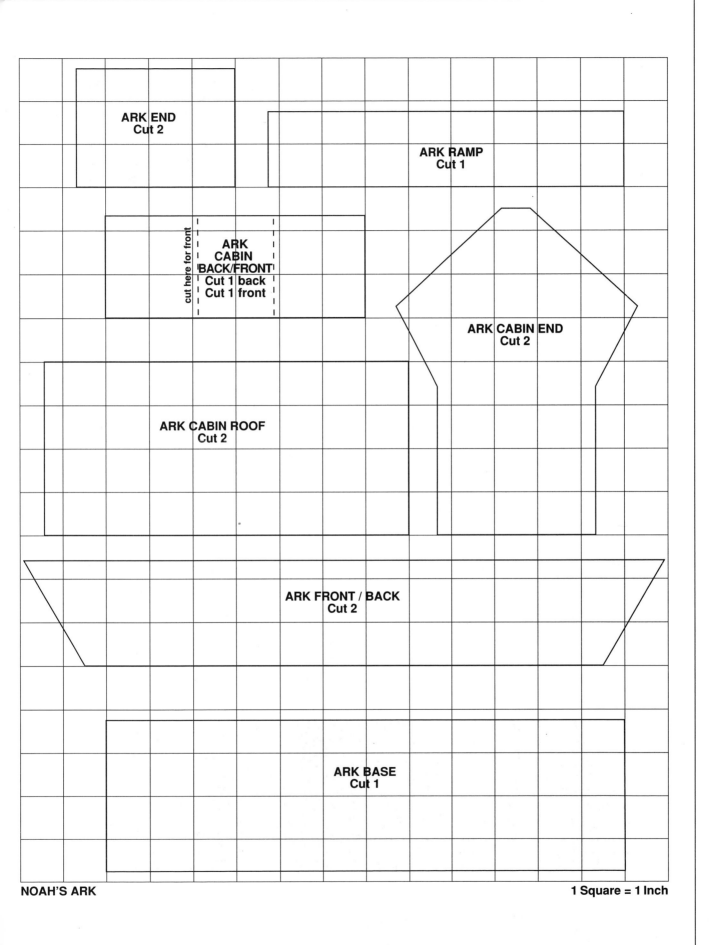

ARK END
Cut 2

ARK RAMP
Cut 1

cut here for front

ARK
CABIN
BACK/FRONT
Cut 1 back
Cut 1 front

ARK CABIN END
Cut 2

ARK CABIN ROOF
Cut 2

ARK FRONT / BACK
Cut 2

ARK BASE
Cut 1

NOAH'S ARK

1 Square = 1 Inch

CHERRY DIVINITY

Pictured on page 87.

INGREDIENTS

2½ cups sugar
½ cup light corn syrup
½ cup water
2 egg whites
½ teaspoon cherry extract
1 or 2 drops red food coloring
½ cup finely chopped candied cherries

METHOD

Mix sugar, corn syrup, and water in a heavy 2-quart saucepan. Cover and stir over medium-high heat till the mixture boils. Clip a candy thermometer to side of pan. Reduce heat to medium; continue cooking, without stirring, till thermometer registers 260°, hard-ball stage (10 to 15 minutes).

Remove saucepan from heat; remove thermometer. In a large mixing bowl, beat egg whites with a sturdy, freestanding electric mixer on medium speed till stiff peaks form (tips stand straight). Gradually pour hot mixture in a thin stream over whites, beating on high speed about 3 minutes; scrape sides of bowl occasionally. Add cherry extract and food coloring. Continue beating on high just till candy starts to lose its gloss. When beaters are lifted, mixture should fall in a ribbon that mounds on itself. This should take 5 to 6 minutes.

Drop a spoonful of candy mixture onto waxed paper. If it stays mounded, the mixture has been beaten sufficiently. Immediately stir in cherries. Quickly drop remaining mixture from a teaspoon onto waxed paper. If mixture flattens, beat ½ to 1 minute more; check again. If mixture is too stiff to spoon, beat in a few drops hot water till candy is a softer consistency. Store tightly covered. Makes about 40 pieces.

MAKING DIVINITY

1. Beat egg whites with a freestanding electric mixer on medium speed till stiff peaks form.

2. Gradually pour hot mixture in a thin stream over whites, beating on high speed about 3 minutes.

3. Add extract and coloring, then beat on high till mixture, when beaters are lifted, falls in a ribbon.

4. Drop mixture, by spoonfuls, onto waxed paper. If it stays mounded, it has been beaten sufficiently.

MINT DIVINITY

Pictured on page 87.

INGREDIENTS

2½ cups sugar
½ cup light corn syrup
½ cup water
2 egg whites
½ teaspoon mint extract
1 or 2 drops green food coloring

METHOD

Mix sugar, corn syrup, and water in a heavy 2-quart saucepan. Cover and stir over medium-high heat till the mixture boils. Clip a candy thermometer to side of pan. Reduce heat to medium; continue cooking, without stirring, till thermometer registers 260°, hard-ball stage (10 to 15 minutes).

Remove saucepan from heat; remove thermometer. In a large mixing bowl, beat egg whites with a sturdy, freestanding electric mixer on medium speed till stiff peaks form (tips stand straight). Gradually pour hot mixture in a thin stream over whites, beating on high speed about 3 minutes; scrape sides of bowl occasionally. Add mint extract and food coloring. Continue beating on high just till candy starts to lose its gloss. When beaters are lifted, mixture should fall in a ribbon that mounds on itself. This final beating should take 5 to 6 minutes.

Drop a spoonful of candy mixture onto waxed paper. If it stays mounded, the mixture has been beaten sufficiently. Quickly drop remaining mixture from a teaspoon onto waxed paper. If mixture flattens, beat ½ to 1 minute more; check again. If mixture is too stiff to spoon, beat in a few drops hot water till candy is a softer consistency. Store tightly covered. Makes about 40 pieces.

EASY CHOCOLATE-ALMOND TRUFFLES

Pictured on page 87.

INGREDIENTS

1   11½-ounce package milk-chocolate pieces
⅓   cup whipping cream
¼   teaspoon almond extract
⅔   cup toasted ground almonds
4   2-ounce squares vanilla-flavored candy coating
½   cup semisweet chocolate pieces, melted

METHOD

In a heavy saucepan, combine milk-chocolate pieces and whipping cream. Cook over low heat for 4 to 5 minutes or till chocolate melts, stirring frequently. Remove from heat. Cool slightly. Stir in almond extract. Beat with an electric mixer on low speed till smooth. Cover and refrigerate 1 hour or till firm.

Shape chocolate mixture into ¾-inch balls; roll in ground almonds. Place on waxed paper-lined baking sheet. Freeze for 30 minutes. Meanwhile, in a heavy medium saucepan, melt candy coating over low heat, stirring constantly. Quickly dip truffles into melted candy coating, allowing excess coating to drip off. Place truffles on waxed paper and let stand about 30 minutes or till coating is set. Decoratively drizzle the melted semisweet chocolate over tops of truffles. Store in a tightly covered container in the refrigerator. Makes about 2½ dozen truffles.

MAKING TRUFFLES

1. Shape truffle mixture into balls; roll in ground almonds. Place on waxed paper-lined baking sheet to freeze.

2. In a heavy medium saucepan, melt candy coating over low heat, stirring constantly.

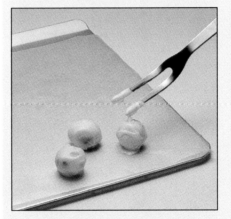

3. Quickly dip truffles into melted candy coating, allowing excess to drip off. Set on lined baking sheet.

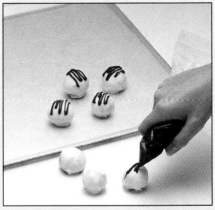

4. When coating is set, drizzle melted semisweet chocolate over the tops of the truffles.

GRANDMA'S FUDGE

Pictured on page 87.

INGREDIENTS

3   tablespoons margarine or butter
3   tablespoons unsweetened cocoa powder
2½   cups sugar
¼   cup plus 2 tablespoons evaporated milk
1   teaspoon light corn syrup

METHOD

In a 2-quart heavy saucepan, melt margarine or butter. Add unsweetened cocoa powder; stir till combined. Add sugar, evaporated milk, and light corn syrup. Cook over medium-high heat till mixture is boiling, stirring constantly with a wooden spoon to dissolve sugar. (This should take about 5 minutes.) Avoid splashing the candy mixture onto sides of pan.

When the mixture starts to boil, carefully clip a candy thermometer to the side of saucepan. Reduce heat to medium-low. The mixture should continue to boil at a moderate, steady rate over the entire surface.

Cook, stirring frequently, for 10 to 15 minutes or till the thermometer registers 230°.

Remove candy thermometer. Pour fudge mixture into a large mixing bowl, but do not scrape saucepan.

MAKING FUDGE

1. When mixture starts to boil, clip a candy thermometer to the pan; boil at steady rate over entire surface.

2. Use a wooden spoon to beat cooled mixture about 7 minutes or till fudge is like soft frosting.

3. Drop mixture by spoonfuls onto baking sheet or pour mixture into pan instead.

Place thermometer in the bowl. Cool till thermometer registers 100° and the mixture is thick. (Depending on the room temperature, this can take between 1 and 2 hours, so check the thermometer frequently.) Do not scrape the bowl or stir during cooling.

Meanwhile, line a baking sheet with waxed paper. (Beginning fudge makers may want to line a 9x5x3-inch loaf pan with aluminum foil, extending the foil over the edges of pan; butter the foil.) Set aside.

Using a wooden spoon, beat the cooled mixture about 7 minutes or till the fudge becomes like a soft frosting. The mixture should start to thicken and hold a swirl, yet still be glossy. Immediately drop the mixture by the teaspoonfuls onto buttered foil or waxed paper (with the help of an assistant). If the fudge starts to set before all of the candy is dropped, stir in ½ teaspoon hot water and continue dropping the fudge. (Beginning fudge makers may want to pour the mixture into the loaf pan instead of dropping it.) When the fudge is firm, lift it out of the pan and cut it into squares.

Cover the fudge; store in a cool, dry place up to one week. Makes about 30 pieces.

VICTORIAN STEAMED PUDDING

Pictured on page 88.

INGREDIENTS

1¼	cups all-purpose flour
1	teaspoon baking powder
½	teaspoon baking soda
½	teaspoon ground cinnamon
½	teaspoon ground nutmeg
2	eggs
¾	cup packed brown sugar
½	cup shortening
2	medium carrots, sliced
1	medium apple, peeled, cored, and cut into eighths
1	medium potato, peeled and cut into pieces
¾	cup raisins
2	tablespoons orange liqueur (optional)
1	3-ounce package cream cheese
¼	cup margarine or butter
½	teaspoon finely shredded orange peel
1	cup sifted powdered sugar
2	tablespoons orange juice

METHOD

Combine the flour, baking powder, baking soda, ground cinnamon, and the ground nutmeg in a large mixing bowl; set aside.

Place eggs, brown sugar, and shortening in a blender container or food processor bowl. Cover and blend or process till smooth.

Add the sliced carrots; blend or process till chopped. Add the peeled apple; blend or process till chopped. Add the peeled potato; blend or process till finely chopped. Stir the carrot-apple-potato mixture and the raisins into dry ingredients.

Pour batter into a greased and floured 6½-cup tower mold (without the tube); cover tightly with greased foil.

Set the mold inside the crockery liner of a 3½-, 4-, or 6-quart crockery cooker. Cover and cook on high-heat setting for 4 hours.

Remove the mold from the cooker. Cool 10 minutes.

Unmold the pudding. If desired, brush the pudding with orange liqueur. Let the pudding stand 20 to 30 minutes before serving.

For the pudding sauce, in a small bowl beat the cream cheese and margarine or butter till light and fluffy. Slowly beat in the powdered sugar. Stir in the orange juice till smooth. Drizzle some of the cream cheese sauce over the pudding. Pass the remaining sauce. Makes 6 to 8 servings.

Family
Celebrations

*The true spirit of Christmas fills the air when we're with family—
sharing laughter, fine foods, and decorations. This year, enliven
your celebration with brunch, a light supper, or some peppermint
treats from the recipes and trims in this festive collection.*

PHOTOGRAPHER: HOPKINS ASSOCIATES

Christmas Morning Buffet

Put holiday rise-and-shine into your Christmas morning and gather the whole family around a brunch that's as festive and extraordinary as the day itself. Make French toast the star attraction with a luscious topping of strawberries. (It's surprisingly quick to fix.) Then complement it with a spinach salad, ornamented in bright Mandarin orange slices and a strawberry-orange salad dressing. For both recipes, turn to page 108.

PHOTOGRAPHER: HOPKINS
ASSOCIATES

Candy-Stripes Place Setting

All set for the holidays? Look at this red-and-white striped explosion of candy-cane delights. These easy ideas include everything from an appliquéd place mat and a licorice-stitched place card to a candy-cane container and a tumbler coaster. Serve up one place setting for Santa's once-a-year visit or make a tableful for a child's Christmas party or gala family gathering.
Instructions begin on page 108.

DESIGNER: DONNA CHESNUT ● PHOTOGRAPHER: SCOTT LITTLE

Candy-Cane Cake

Don't set out cookies for Santa tonight. Instead, fill his tummy with this yummy Christmas treat. A classic favorite, our red cocoa cake is topped with snowy frosting and a sprinkling of crushed peppermint pieces. For the recipe, see page 110.

PHOTOGRAPHER: SCOTT LITTLE

Christmas Dinner Bells

Let a melody of heavenly bells add its own sweet harmony to your family's Christmas Eve supper. The fare is a trio medley that includes oyster stew with vegetables, Christmas bell bread—a yeast recipe that rings with orange peel and cinnamon flavors—and apricot Bavarian crème with raspberry sauce. Crocheted bells serve as lacy grace notes tied to golden flatware and holiday packages, and later to the branches of your tree. Then repeat the sounding joy all over your tabletop with a scattering of antique or new bells and bell-trimmed greeting cards. Recipes begin on page 110, bell instructions on page 111.

DESIGNER: JOAN G. GLASS
PHOTOGRAPHER: HOPKINS
ASSOCIATES

108

ORANGE-SPINACH TOSS

Pictured on page 103.

INGREDIENTS

- 8 cups torn, prewashed spinach or mixed salad greens
- 1 11-ounce can Mandarin orange sections
- ¼ of an 8-ounce container (¼ cup) soft-style cream cheese with strawberries
- ⅓ cup orange juice
- ½ cup cashews or dry-roasted peanuts

METHOD

Place salad greens in a large salad bowl. Open the Mandarin oranges and drain the liquid. Add the drained orange sections to the spinach. Carefully toss. Set aside.

For salad dressing, put the cream cheese in a small mixing bowl. Add orange juice and stir to combine with a wire whisk or fork. Pour dressing over spinach and oranges. Toss again.

Sprinkle cashews or dry-roasted peanuts over salad before serving. Makes 8 servings.

STRAWBERRY FRENCH TOAST

Pictured on pages 102–103.

INGREDIENTS

- 8 slices French bread, cut 1½ inches thick
- 5 eggs
- ¾ cup milk
- 1 teaspoon vanilla extract
- 5 cups loose-pack frozen strawberries or raspberries
- ⅔ cup sugar
- ½ teaspoon cinnamon

METHOD

Break the eggs into a large mixing bowl and stir them till they are all one color. Stir in the milk and the vanilla.

Dip the French bread slices into the egg mixture for about 30 seconds on each side. Place the bread slices on a baking sheet and let stand for about 10 minutes till egg mixture is absorbed.

Heat oven to 450°. Grease a 13x9x1½-inch glass baking dish. Spread frozen strawberries evenly over bottom of dish.

In a small bowl combine sugar and cinnamon. Sprinkle ½ cup of the sugar mixture over the strawberries. With a spatula carefully place bread slices over the strawberries. Sprinkle remaining sugar over the bread. Bake for 15 minutes till bread is golden brown. (Bake for 5 minutes more, if necessary.)

To serve, use a spatula to place one slice of bread on a plate, then spoon some of the strawberries and syrup on top. Makes 8 servings.

CANDY-STRIPES PLACE SETTING ACCESSORIES

As shown on page 104, the candy-cane wreath coaster measures approximately 3½ inches in diameter and 1⅜ inches high; the candy-cane favor box measures approximately 3¾x3½x2 inches; the licorice-trimmed place card, folded, measures 2½x4 inches.

MATERIALS

COASTER

Three 3½-inch-diameter candy wreaths

½ yard of ¼-inch-wide red satin ribbon

½ yard of ¼-inch-wide green satin ribbon

FAVOR BOX

Small pudding box

Hole punch

Red tinsel stem

Thirty-three 3½-inch-long peppermint sticks

Hot-glue gun; glue sticks

Red tinsel package stuffing

Assorted candies

PLACE CARD

5x6-inch piece of white heavy paper stock

Hole punch

Red licorice strips

Hot-glue gun; glue sticks

Felt-tip marker

INSTRUCTIONS

For the coaster, stack three candy-cane wreaths, one on top of the other. Cut the red and green satin ribbon lengths in half. Tie candy-cane wreaths together on each side using the red ribbon. Then tie wreaths together a second time, using the green ribbon and placing a green ribbon next to each red ribbon. Slip glass into coaster.

For the favor box, cut away the top from a small pudding box. Punch a hole in each narrow side close to the top edge to receive the handle. Twist each end of the tinsel stem through the holes. To cover the bottom of the box, hot-glue four peppermint sticks, side by side and parallel with the long edge of the box bottom. The peppermint sticks should extend about ¼ inch over each short end. Hot-glue 27 of the remaining 29 peppermint sticks, side by side and parallel with the long edges of the box front, back, and sides. Glue the remaining two peppermint sticks to each long edge of the box bottom. Fill half of the box with red tinsel package stuffing, then fill to the top with assorted candies.

For the place card, fold the paper in half crosswise so it measures 3x5 inches. Mark dots with a pencil for placement of holes around the outside edge (on the front of the folded card only). Refer to the photograph on page 104 for number of holes and placement. Punch holes in place card. Thread licorice up from the back at the top left hole. Lace licorice in and out of the holes all around the place card, ending on the back side. Hot-glue loose ends to back of card. Tie a licorice bow and hot-glue it to the card in the top left corner. Write name on card with a felt-tip marker.

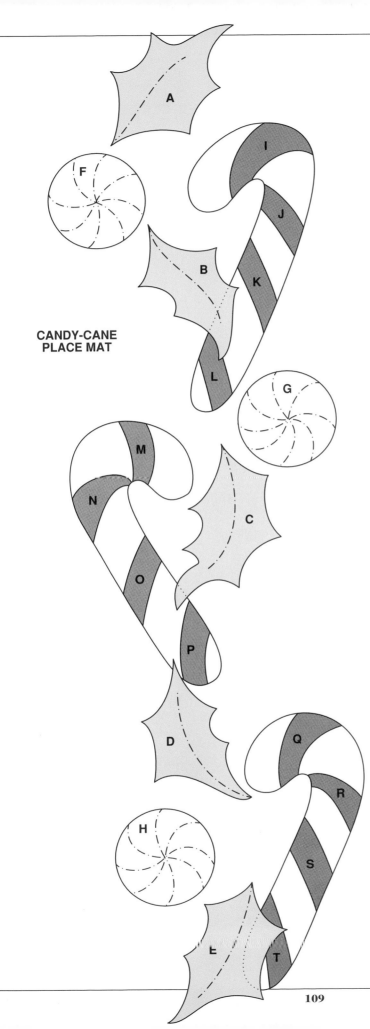

CANDY-CANE PLACE MAT

CANDY-CANE-AND-HOLLY PLACE MAT

As shown on page 104, place mat measures 12½x18½ inches.

MATERIALS

For one place mat

Tracing paper
Black permanent marking pen
Paper-backed iron-on adhesive
5x9-inch piece of white fabric for candy canes and peppermint drops
6x6-inch piece of green print fabric for holly leaves
6x6-inch piece of red pin-dot fabric for candy-cane stripes
12x18-inch piece of white-on-white print fabric for place mat
Fabric marking pen
Sewing threads to match fabrics
12x18-inch piece of fleece
12x18-inch piece of white broadcloth
2 yards of ½-inch-wide flat red trim
24 red 4-millimeter beads
12 green 4-millimeter beads

INSTRUCTIONS

Trace the complete design, *left,* onto tracing paper using a black permanent marking pen. Place the iron-on adhesive, paper side up, atop the tracing-paper pattern; trace around the peppermint drops, the holly leaves, the complete candy canes, and the individual candy-cane stripes. Label these traced shapes with an R to designate the right border.

Turn the original tracing-paper pattern over and trace the shapes onto the iron-on adhesive again; this time, label the traced shapes with an L to designate the left border. Cut out all of the pieces.

Following the manufacturer's instructions, fuse the candy canes and peppermint drops to the white fabric, the holly leaves to the green print, and the candy-cane stripes to the red pin-dot fabric. Cut out all of the shapes.

For ease in placement of the appliqués, first mark the 12x18-inch white-on-white place mat with a ¼-inch seam allowance (the seam allowance *is included* in measurement). Slip traced pattern beneath rectangle. Place design about ¾ inch from seam line on each side.

Pin appliqué pieces in place along right and left sides of the white-on-white print rectangle, reversing the pattern for the left side. Remove pins from pieces one by one, remove paper backing, reposition, and fuse in place. Fuse stripes to candy canes last. Mark spiral lines on the peppermint drops with the fabric marking pen.

Work a machine zigzag-appliqué stitch around the edges of the leaves with green thread, and around the candy canes, candy-cane stripes, and peppermint drops with red thread. Stitch along marked spiral lines with red thread.

Lay appliquéd place mat over the fleece; baste layers together around perimeter ¼ inch from edge. With right sides facing, sew place mat front to back, leaving an opening for turning. Trim corners and turn right side out. Slip-stitch opening closed. Edge mat with red trim.

Sew beads in groups of three to base of each holly leaf, using green beads for two leaves on each side and red for the remaining leaves. Sew a single red bead to the center of each peppermint drop.

CANDY-CANE CAKE
Pictured on page 105.

INGREDIENTS
- 2¼ cups sifted cake flour
- ½ cup unsweetened cocoa powder
- ½ teaspoon salt
- ½ cup shortening
- 1½ cups granulated sugar
- 1 teaspoon vanilla
- 2 eggs
- 2 ounces red food coloring (¼ cup)
- 1 cup buttermilk
- 1 teaspoon baking soda
- 1 teaspoon vinegar
- Cream Cheese Frosting
- Crushed peppermint candy

METHOD
Grease and flour two 9x1½-inch round baking pans or one 13x9x2-inch baking pan. In a small mixing bowl stir together the flour, cocoa powder, and salt. Set pans and flour mixture aside.

Beat the shortening with an electric mixer on medium to high speed in a large mixing bowl for about 30 seconds or till softened. Add the sugar and vanilla to the shortening and beat till mixture is well combined.

Add eggs, one at a time, beating on medium speed after each addition. Beat in the food coloring on low speed.

Alternately add the flour mixture and the buttermilk, beating on low to medium speed after each addition just till combined.

Stir together the baking soda and the vinegar. Add to the batter, mixing till combined.

Pour batter into prepared pans. Bake in 350° oven for 30 to 35 minutes (about 30 minutes for the 13x9x2-inch pan) or till a wooden toothpick inserted near the center of each cake comes out clean. Cool the cake layers in the pans for 10 minutes.

Remove cake layers from the pans and completely cool on wire racks. If using a 13x9x2-inch pan, do not remove cake layer from the pan. Completely cool it in the pan on a wire rack.

Frost with Cream Cheese Frosting *(recipe below)*. If desired, decorate top of cake with crushed peppermint candy. Cover and store in the refrigerator for up to 3 days. Makes 12 servings.

Cream Cheese Frosting: In a medium saucepan, and using a whisk, blend *1 cup milk* into *3 tablespoons all-purpose flour*. Cook and stir over medium heat till thickened and bubbly.

Reduce heat; cook and stir for 2 minutes more. Cover the surface with plastic wrap. Cool to room temperature (do not stir).

In a mixing bowl, beat *1 cup softened butter* (do not use butter substitutes), *1 cup granulated sugar,* and *1 teaspoon vanilla* with an electric mixer on medium speed till light and fluffy.

Add the cooled cooked mixture to the butter mixture ¼ cup at a time, beating on low speed after each addition till smooth. Spread over cooled cake.

APRICOT BAVARIAN CRÈME WITH RASPBERRY SAUCE
Pictured on page 106.

INGREDIENTS
- ½ cup sugar
- 1 envelope unflavored gelatin
- 1 5½-ounce can apricot nectar
- 1 cup whipping cream
- 1 teaspoon vanilla
- 1 8-ounce carton low-fat vanilla yogurt
- 1 10-ounce package frozen raspberries, thawed
- 2 tablespoons powdered sugar
- 1 tablespoon orange juice

METHOD
Using a saucepan, combine sugar and gelatin. Stir in apricot nectar. Cook and stir over medium heat till sugar and gelatin dissolve.

Stir in the whipping cream and vanilla. Gradually whisk the vanilla yogurt into the gelatin mixture till well combined.

Pour the mixture into lightly oiled ⅓ cup individual bell-shaped molds. Cover and chill for 8 to 24 hours or till firm.

To serve, unmold onto a serving dish. Top with Raspberry Sauce *(recipe below)*. Makes 6 servings.

Raspberry Sauce: In a blender container or a food processor bowl combine the thawed raspberries, the powdered sugar, and the orange juice.

Cover and blend or process till smooth. Press through a sieve to remove seeds; discard seeds.

CHRISTMAS BELL BREAD

Pictured on pages 106–107.

INGREDIENTS

- 2½ to 3 cups all-purpose flour
- 1 package active dry yeast
- ⅔ cup milk
- ¼ cup sugar
- ¼ cup margarine or butter
- ¼ teaspoon salt
- 1 egg
- ½ teaspoon finely shredded orange peel
- ¼ cup sugar
- 1½ teaspoons finely shredded orange peel
- ¼ teaspoon ground cinnamon
- 1 tablespoon melted margarine or butter
- Orange Icing
- Candied cherries, halved

METHOD

In a small mixing bowl, stir together *1¼ cups of the flour* and the yeast. Set aside. In a small saucepan, heat and stir the milk, the ¼ cup sugar, the ¼ cup margarine or butter, and the salt till warm (120° to 130°) and the margarine is almost melted. Add milk mixture to flour mixture; add egg and the ½ teaspoon orange peel.

Beat with an electric mixer on low speed for 30 seconds, scraping bowl frequently. Beat on high speed for 3 minutes. Using a spoon, stir in as much remaining flour as you can.

Turn dough out onto a lightly floured surface. Knead in enough of the remaining flour to make a moderately stiff dough that is smooth and elastic (6 to 8 minutes total). Shape into a ball. Place in a lightly greased bowl; turn once to grease surface. Cover and let rise in a warm place till double (about 60 minutes). (Or, cover and let rise in the refrigerator overnight.)

Punch dough down. Turn out onto a lightly floured surface. Remove one piece of dough, about the size of a walnut, and set aside. Cover both portions of dough and let rest for 10 minutes.

Combine the ¼ cup sugar, 1½ teaspoons orange peel, and the cinnamon. Roll out larger portion of dough to a 10-inch circle. Transfer to a greased baking sheet. Brush with some of the melted butter. Sprinkle with the sugar mixture.

To shape bell, form smaller piece of dough into a ball; moisten the bottom and place it on the bottom of the circle to form the clapper. Fold in the sides of the circle, overlapping slightly at the top. Brush bell and clapper with the remaining melted margarine. Cover and let rise in a warm place till almost double (about 30 minutes). (Allow longer if dough has been chilled.) Bake in 350° oven for 15 minutes. Cover with foil and bake for 10 minutes more or till golden brown. Transfer to wire rack to cool.

Drizzle or spread with Orange Icing and arrange candied cherry halves to garnish. Makes 1 bell bread with 16 to 20 servings.

Orange Icing: Combine *1 cup sifted powdered sugar* and *½ teaspoon vanilla.* Stir in enough *orange juice (2 to 3 teaspoons)* to make an icing of drizzling consistency. Makes about ½ cup.

OYSTER STEW WITH VEGETABLES

Pictured on pages 106–107. Use 5-quart Dutch oven to double recipe.

INGREDIENTS

- ½ of a 16-ounce package frozen mixed broccoli, cauliflower, and carrots (about 2 cups)
- 1 small onion, cut into thin wedges
- ½ cup water
- ½ teaspoon instant chicken bouillon granules
- ⅛ teaspoon ground white pepper
- 1 bay leaf
- 2 13-ounce cans (3½ cups total) evaporated skimmed milk
- 1 pint shucked oysters or two 8-ounce cans whole oysters

METHOD

Cut up any large vegetables. In a 3-quart saucepan combine the vegetables, onion, water, bouillon granules, white pepper, and the bay leaf. Bring to a boil. Reduce heat. Cover and simmer for 5 to 7 minutes or till the vegetables are crisp-tender. Do not drain.

Stir in the evaporated milk. Heat all the way through. Add the undrained oysters to the vegetable mixture. Cook over a medium heat for about 5 minutes or till the edges of the oysters curl, stirring frequently. (If using canned oysters, just heat through.) Remove the bay leaf. Makes 6 servings.

CROCHETED ANTIQUE BELL

Shown on page 107, the bell is 3 inches tall. Crochet abbreviations are on page 158.

MATERIALS

Size 9 steel crochet hook
J.P. Coats Metallic Knit-Cro-Sheen (100-yard ball): white (1G)
½-inch-diameter wood bead
White glue

INSTRUCTIONS

Ch 6, join with sl st to form ring.
Rnd 1: Ch 4, * dc in ring, ch 1 *. Rep bet *s 18 more times. Join last ch-1 in third ch of first ch-4.
Rnd 2: Ch 3, dc in ch-1 sp, * dc in dc, dc in ch-1 sp *. Rep bet *s 18 more times. Join in top of first ch-3.
Rnd 3: Ch 4, sk next dc, * dc in dc, ch 1, sk next dc *. Rep bet *s 18 more times. Join last ch-1 in third ch of first ch-4—20 filet sps.
Rnd 4: Ch 5, * dc in next dc, ch 2 *. Rep bet *s around. Join last ch-2 in third ch of first ch-5.
Rnd 5: Rep Rnd 4.
Rnd 6: Ch 5, dc in dc, ch 2, dc in dc, 2 dc in ch-2 sp, dc in dc, ch 2, * dc in dc, ch 2, dc in dc, ch 2, 2 dc in ch-2 sp, dc in dc, ch 2 *. Rep bet *s 3 more times. Join last ch-2 in third ch of first ch-5.

Antique Bell

Rnd 7: Sl st in ch-2 sp, ch 4, trc, ch 3, **holding last st on hook, in same sp work 2 trc, yo, thread through all 3 sts–2 trc-cl made;** ch 7, * sk to center bl of open filet, 2 trc-cl, ch 3, 2 trc-cl in same sp, ch 7 *. Rep bet *s 3 more times. Join last ch-7 in trc of first cl, sl st in next 2 chs.

Rnd 8: Ch 3, dc, ch 3, 2 dc-cl in same st, ch 3, sk to fourth ch of ch-7 of prev rnd, then 6 dc in same sp, ch 3; * 2 dc-cl in center ch of next ch-3, ch 3, 2 dc-cl in same sp, ch 3, sk to center ch of next ch-7, 6 dc in same sp, ch 3 *. Rep bet *s 3 more times. Join last ch-3 in top of first ch-3.

Rnd 9: Sl st past the 2 sets of 2 dc-cl to center ch of ch-3; * ch 4, 3 trc-cl, only work each trc in first 3 dc, yo, thread through all 4 sts, ch 5, 3 trc-cl in next 3 dc, ch 4, sc in center ch of ch-3 *. Rep bet *s 4 more times. Join last ch-4 in base of first ch-4.

Rnd 10: Ch 7, * 1 dc, ch 3, dc in third ch of ch-5, ch 7, sc in next sc *. Rep bet *s 4 more times. Join last ch-7 in base of first ch-7.

Rnd 11: * Ch 5, sc in next dc, (ch 4, sc in fourth ch from hook–picot made). Rep bet ( )s 2 more times, sc in next dc, ch 5, sc in next sc *. Rep bet *s around. Fasten off.

Hanging loop: Attach thread on top of bell, ch 12, sl st to opposite side in ring, ch 1, turn, sc over ch to beg. Sl st in first ch, fasten off. Weave threads into work.

Clapper: Ch 4, work 6 dc in fourth ch from hook, join in top of first ch-4.

Rnd 2: Ch 3, dc in same sp, 2 dc in each dc around. Join in top of first ch-3.

Rnd 3: Ch 3, dc in each dc around. Join in top of first ch-3. Insert bead.

Rnd 4: Stretch crochet work over bead, ch about 1½ inches, leaving a 2-inch thread to tie to hanging loop when bell is stiffened and finished.

Stiffening: Use two parts white glue mixed with one part water for a stiffening solution. Wash crochet work in cold-water detergent; rinse well. Press almost dry in terry-cloth towel. Stack several small paper cups, making stack slightly taller than bell. Cover stack with plastic wrap, inserting one more cup in bottom of stack to hold plastic wrap in place. For rounded top on bell, place several cotton balls on top of cup before covering with plastic wrap. Stretch damp crochet over stack. Paint stiffening solution on work, beginning at hanging loop and working down. Saturate crochet. Place on heavy cardboard

covered with wax paper. If bell has points, pin them to cardboard using rust-proof pins. Allow to partially dry; twist bell and remove it from cups, wipe away excess stiffening solution, and place back on cups. (This helps prevent webbing of solution between openings of crochet.) When completely dry, remove cups; twist plastic wrap away from inside of bell.

Finishing: When bell is dry, insert crochet hook inside bell from the top. Pull clapper thread through, wind around the hanging loop several times, then secure in place.

CROCHETED INSPIRATION BELL

Shown on page 107, the bell is 3 inches tall.

MATERIALS
Size 9 crochet hook
J.P. Coats Metallic Knit-Cro-Sheen (100-yard ball): white (1G)
½-inch-diameter wood bead
White glue

INSTRUCTIONS
Ch 6, join with sl st to form ring.
Rnd 1: Ch 4, * dc in ring, ch 1 *. Rep bet *s 10 more times. Join last

Inspiration Bell

ch-1 in third ch of first ch-4—12 dc, with ch-1 bet.

Rnd 2: Ch 5, * dc in dc, ch 2 *. Rep bet *s 10 more times. Join last ch-2 in third ch of first ch-5.

Rnd 3: Ch 3, 2 dc in ch-2 sp, * dc in dc, 2 dc in ch-2 sp *. Rep bet *s 10 more times. Join in top of first ch-3—36 dc.

Rnd 4: Ch 4, trc in same sp, ch 5, sk next 5 dc, **holding last st on hook of each trc, 2 trc in next dc, yo, thread through all 3 sts—2 trc-clusters made,** ch 6, sl st in trc-cl joining—ch-lp made, ch 5, * sk next 5 dc, 2 trc-cl in next dc, ch 6, sl st in trc-cl joining—ch-6 lp made, ch 5 *. Rep bet *s 4 more times. Join last ch-5 in top of first ch-4, ch 6, sl st in base of same ch-6, sl st to third ch of next ch-5.

Rnd 5: * Ch 2, (2 trc-cl in ch-6 lp, ch 3, 2 trc-cl in same lp, ch 3, 2 trc-cl in same lp, ch 2), sc in third ch of next ch-5 of prev rnd *. Rep bet *s 5 more times. Join last ch-2 in base of first ch-2. Sl st to second trc-cl, and sc in top of cl.

Rnd 6: * Ch 8, sl st in top of next center trc-cl *. Rep bet *s around. Join last ch-8 in base of first ch-8.

Rnd 7: * Ch 5, sk 2 ch, sc in next ch, ch 5, sk 2 ch, sc in next ch, ch 5, sk 2 ch, sc in sc. Rep bet *s around. *Last lp:* Ch 2, dc in base of first ch-5; hook in center of lp. *Note:* Because hook is in center of lp you are ready to begin next rnd.

Rnd 8: * Ch 5, sc in next lp *. Rep bet *s around. *Last lp:* Ch 2, dc in base of first ch-5. Hook in center of lp.

Rnd 9: * Ch 2, sc in next lp *. Rep bet *s around. Join last ch-2 in base of first ch-2.

Rnd 10: Sl st in next 2 chs and next sc. Ch 4, trc in same sp, ch 9, * sk (2 ch, sc, 2 ch, sc, 2 ch), then 2 trc-cl in next sc, ch 6, sl st in base of same ch-6, ch 9 *. Rep bet *s 5 more times. Last ch-9 is joined in top of first ch-4, ch 6, sl st in base of ch-6, sl st to fifth ch of ch-9 of prev rnd.

Rnd 11: Rep Rnd 5, except sc in fifth ch of ch-9 of prev rnd. Join in base of first ch-2. Fasten off.

Joyful Bell

Make hanging loop and clapper, stiffen the bell, and finish as directed for the Crocheted Antique Bell on page 112.

CROCHETED JOYFUL BELL

Shown on page 107, the bell is 3 inches tall.

MATERIALS
Size 9 steel crochet hook
J.P. Coats Metallic Knit-Cro-Sheen
(100-yard ball): white (1G)
½-inch-diameter wood bead
White glue

INSTRUCTIONS
Ch 6, join with sl st to form ring.

Rnd 1: Ch 4, * dc in ring, ch 1 *. Rep bet *s 10 more times. Join last ch-1 in third ch of first ch-4—12 dc with ch-1 bet.

Rnd 2: Ch 5, * dc in dc, ch 2 *. Rep bet *s 10 more times. Join last ch-2 in third ch of first ch-5.

Rnd 3: Ch 3, 2 dc in ch-2 sp, * dc in dc, 2 dc in ch-2 sp *. Rep bet *s 10 more times. Join in top of first ch-3.

Rnd 4: * Ch 1, sk 2 dc, (dc, ch 1) 5 times in next dc, sk 2 dc, sc in next dc *. Rep bet *s 5 more times.

Join last ch-1 in base of first ch-1.

Rnd 5: Sl st in third dc, then ch 4, (dc, ch 1) 4 times in same sp; * (dc, ch 1) 5 times in third dc of next shell *. Rep bet *s 4 more times. Join in third ch of first ch-4.

Rnd 6: Rep Rnd 5.

Rnd 7: Rep Rnd 5, except ch 2 bet shells.

Rnd 8: Sl st to third dc, ch 4, (dc, ch 1) 4 times in same sp, ch 4, **hdc in third ch from hook, ch 2, sl st in base of hdc, ch 1—picot made,** * (dc, ch 1) 5 times in third dc of prev rnd, ch 4, picot *. Rep bet *s 4 more times. Join last ch-1 to third ch of first ch-4.

Rnd 9: Ch 5, (dc, ch 1) 4 times in same sp, ch 5, **hdc in third ch from hook, ch 2, sl st in base of hdc, ch 2—picot made,** *(dc, ch 1) 5 times in third dc of prev rnd, ch 5, picot; rep bet *s 4 more times. Join last ch-1 in third ch of first ch-5.

Rnd 10: Sl st to third dc, * ch 4, in same sp (dc, ch 1, dc, ch 2, **hdc in second ch from hook, ch 2, sl st in base of hdc—picot made,** ch 1, dc, ch 1 dc) ch 5, hdc in second ch from hook, ch 2, sl st in base of hdc, ch 3 *. Rep bet *s 5 more times. Fasten off.

Make the loop and the clapper, stiffen, and finish as directed on page 112.

A Collector's Dream

What wondrous whimsical delights dance in your holiday dreams? Is it visions of Santas, angels, and snowmen to add to your collections? Join us as we nod off to this magical playtime place, where dolls, cherubs, roly-poly snowmen, and Santas of every kind pop up at a whim. Then awake and begin creating these beauties with the magic of your handcrafting skills.

Photographer: Hopkins Associates

Sweet Angel Baby

What a little angel! As endearing as a lullaby, this baby doll tugs at the sentimental heartstrings, bringing joy to your hands as you sew her, and hugs and kisses from a special someone on your Christmas list. Christened Angelina Joy, she wears the prettiest holiday dress, pantaloon undies, golden painted-on shoes, and gossamer wings. Her arms and legs are button-joined at the body. A plastic-foam ball covered in knit fabric gives her a perfectly rounded head. For instructions, see page 122. The pattern is on pages 123 and 124.

DESIGNER: PHYLLIS DUNSTAN ● PHOTOGRAPHER: SCOTT LITTLE

Treetop Angel

*O*ne look at Gabriella and her celestial radiance shines right through. She's created with all the details you might imagine in an angelic messenger, from her long wavy tresses and feathery wings to a skirt so billowy it almost lifts her through the air. Glorious among the evergreen boughs, this lovely creature is truly ethereal perched high atop the tree. Instructions begin on page 125.

The pattern is on pages 126 and 127.

DESIGNER: TARESIA BOERNKE ● PHOTOGRAPHER: HOPKINS ASSOCIATES

Frosty, No-Sew Snow Family

Even a sunny face can't melt our frosty, no-sew family. To build these cheery folks, start with a simple construction made of plastic-foam balls, jar lids, and wire. Add just the right touch of frost from purchased white snow paste. Then when the figures dry, dress them up in colorful fleece accessories. Set the trio on your mantel or share them with a friend, and hearts will melt away. Instructions begin on page 127.

DESIGNER: JEFF JULSETH ● PHOTOGRAPHER: HOPKINS ASSOCIATES

Herbal Snowman

*J*ust like the old peddlar with his Christmas pack, this aromatic snowman carries his own collection of goodies. Draped over cinnamon-stick arms, his herbs-and-spice showcase includes dried wheat, eucalyptus, and other garden delights. The elongated snow figure is a stitch-and-stuff construction that's fashioned from tea-dyed muslin. He's a dapper fellow, too, dressed in a woolly scarf and stocking cap.

For instructions and the pattern, see pages 129–130.

DESIGNER: JEFF JULSETH ● PHOTOGRAPHER: HOPKINS ASSOCIATES

Primitive Santa

He's a jolly old elf all right. With outstretched arms and rustic charm, this country moppet grabs your heart and captures every collector's imagination. Styled gnome-like after earliest depictions of our beloved St. Nick, this Santa is unusual, too, because he wears his seams on the outside. A touch of sponge painting, a bit of embroidery, and an overall dye bath in tea makes this Santa an adventure in crafting. Instructions begin on page 130; the pattern is on page 131.

DESIGNER: SUSAN CAGE-KNOCH ● PHOTOGRAPHER: HOPKINS ASSOCIATES

Lovable Elf Santa

Know who's naughty or nice? This little fellow does! And judging by his pleased expression, he's got loads of Christmas wishes to fill. Santa's clothes are made from fabrics rich with pattern, color, and texture, making him a mantel standout. His chubby-cheeked face and hands are stitched in felt. Best of all, jointed arms and legs let you pose him any way you like. The instructions and patterns are on pages 132–136.

DESIGNER: PHYLLIS DUNSTAN
PHOTOGRAPHER: HOPKINS ASSOCIATES

SWEET ANGEL BABY

As shown on pages 115 and 116, angel is 11 inches tall.

MATERIALS

Tracing paper
¼ yard of ecru cotton knit
¼ yard of purple print fabric
5x18-inch piece of purple multi-color print fabric
4x18-inch piece of green-and-white check fabric
Brown paper
1½-inch-diameter plastic-foam ball
Round-head clothespin
Threads to match fabrics
Fabric glue
Polyester fiberfill
Two black glass head pins
Black permanent fine-tip marker
Red fabric crayon
12-inch length of crepe wool hair in desired color
Waxed dental floss
12 inches of ⅜-inch-wide purple satin ribbon for hair bows
Two ½-inch purple star-shaped acrylic stones
Gold metallic thread
8x12-inch piece of green stripe fabric
Gold metallic fabric paint
Small artist's brush
⅓ yard of ⅛-inch-wide gold metallic soutache trim
Two 5-millimeter gold beads
Long soft-sculpture needle
Four ½-inch purple four-hole buttons
Three 4-millimeter beads to coordinate with fabrics
6-inch strand of tiny purple pearl beads
8x8-inch piece of medium-weight interfacing
Iridescent glitter paint

INSTRUCTIONS

Trace patterns for head, neck, body front, and body back, *opposite,* and patterns for pantaloon and sleeve, *page 124,* onto tracing paper; cut out.

Cut head, neck, and body pieces from cotton knit; cut pantaloon and sleeve patterns from purple print. In addition, cut 3¼x18-inch skirt rectangle and 1x8½-inch waistband from purple multicolor print and 2½x18-inch skirt trim strip and two 1½x3-inch sleeve cuffs from green-and-white check fabric. Trace arm pattern, *opposite,* and leg and wings patterns, *page 124,* onto brown paper for templates; cut out.

Patterns include the necessary seam allowances. Sew seams with right sides of fabric facing using ¼-inch seam allowances, unless otherwise indicated. Follow individual instructions closely for construction of body and clothing pieces.

For head, make 1-inch-deep hole in plastic-foam ball using rounded end of clothespin. Sew the three knit head sections together along side seams from dot to dot. Turn right side out. Push plastic-foam ball into knit head through top opening, placing hole in plastic-foam ball at bottom head opening. Glue fabric points to inside of hole.

Stuff two ¾-inch-diameter balls of fiberfill beneath knit on one side of ball to make cheeks. Refer to face diagram, *opposite,* as a guide. Apply glue to top ⅓ of ball and press cotton knit fabric against plastic-foam, smoothing excess fabric toward back and top of head. Cut away excess fabric at top.

Cut away half of pin shaft length from each glass head pin. Dip pins in glue and poke into head for eyes. Using face diagram as guide, draw mouth and brows using the black permanent fine-tip marker. Blush cheeks using red fabric crayon.

Cut the crepe wool hair into two 6-inch lengths. Unbraid and gently pull each strip apart until 1¾ inches wide. Lay strips side by side; stitch across center to make center part. Apply glue to top, sides, and back of head. Position hair on head with stitching running down center from top hairline to base of head; allow glue to dry. Gather hair at each side and tie with dental floss. Cut purple ribbon in half; tie each length into a small bow, trimming away excess. Glue a bow and a purple star stone to each tie. Set head aside.

For body, sew body fronts together along center seam; clip curve.

Lay body front right side up atop right side of one neck piece, overlapping to dotted line; secure with drops of fabric glue. Use a machine zigzag-appliqué stitch and gold metallic thread to cover raw edge. Join body back to remaining neck piece in same manner. Sew body front to back, leaving neck and bottom open as indicated on pattern; turn right side out.

Slip clothespin into neck of body with round part extending above neck opening. Glue neck fabric around clothespin, applying glue exactly ½ inch down from round head. If neck does not fit tightly around pin, make adjustments in neck seams as necessary. When glue is dry, stuff body firmly, keeping clothespin centered. Sew bottom body opening closed.

For legs, draw around leg template two times onto doubled thickness of green stripe; *do not* cut out. Sew along lines, leaving openings as marked on pattern. Cut legs ⅛ inch beyond stitching. Bring back and front seams together at toe and stitch across ⅜ inch from end to shape foot. Turn right side out, stuff, and sew opening closed. Paint shoe gold, following lines shown on pattern. When dry, glue gold trim around dotted line on shoe. Sew gold bead to center top of shoe.

Thread soft-sculpture needle with long doubled strand of dental floss; knot ends. Insert needle at X on one side of body bottom and out at X on opposite side. Push needle through one leg at X and pull so leg is tight against body. Thread button onto needle and sew back through second button hole, through leg, and through body at X. Cut needle from floss, separate floss strands, and knot tightly against body. Rethread needle with both strands and push needle through second leg at X. Bring leg tight against body, thread button onto needle, and sew back through button, leg, and body, exiting behind first leg. Remove needle and separate strands. Pull firmly and make double knot behind first leg. Cut excess floss.

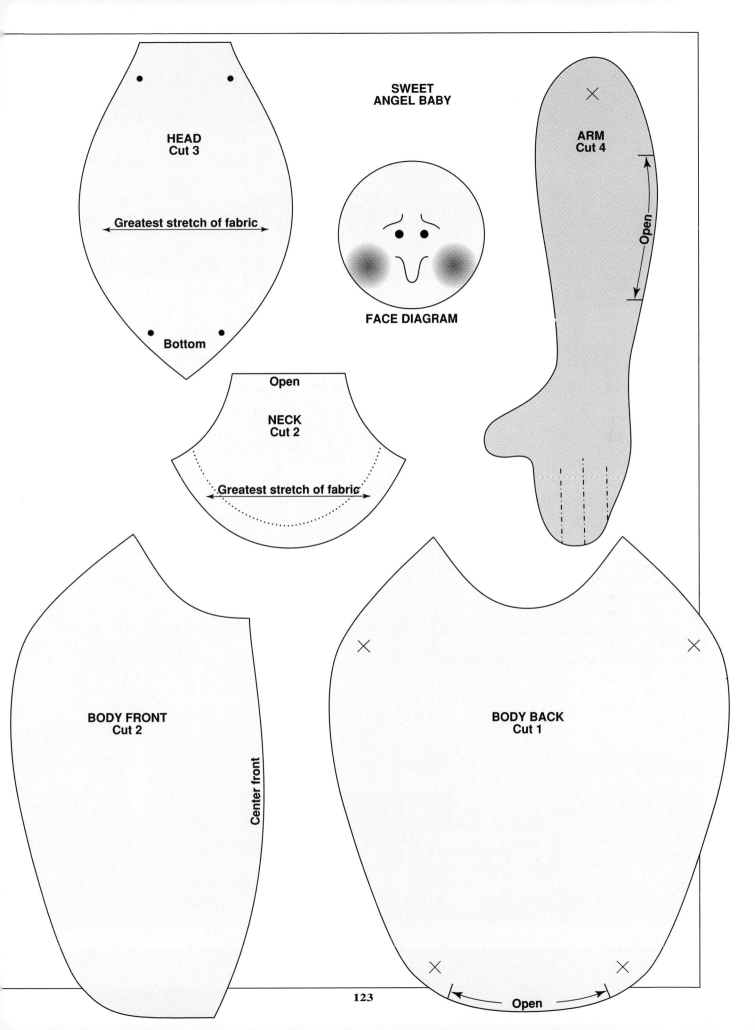

HEAD
Cut 3

Greatest stretch of fabric

Bottom

SWEET
ANGEL BABY

FACE DIAGRAM

ARM
Cut 4

Open

Open

NECK
Cut 2

Greatest stretch of fabric

BODY FRONT
Cut 2

Center front

BODY BACK
Cut 1

Open

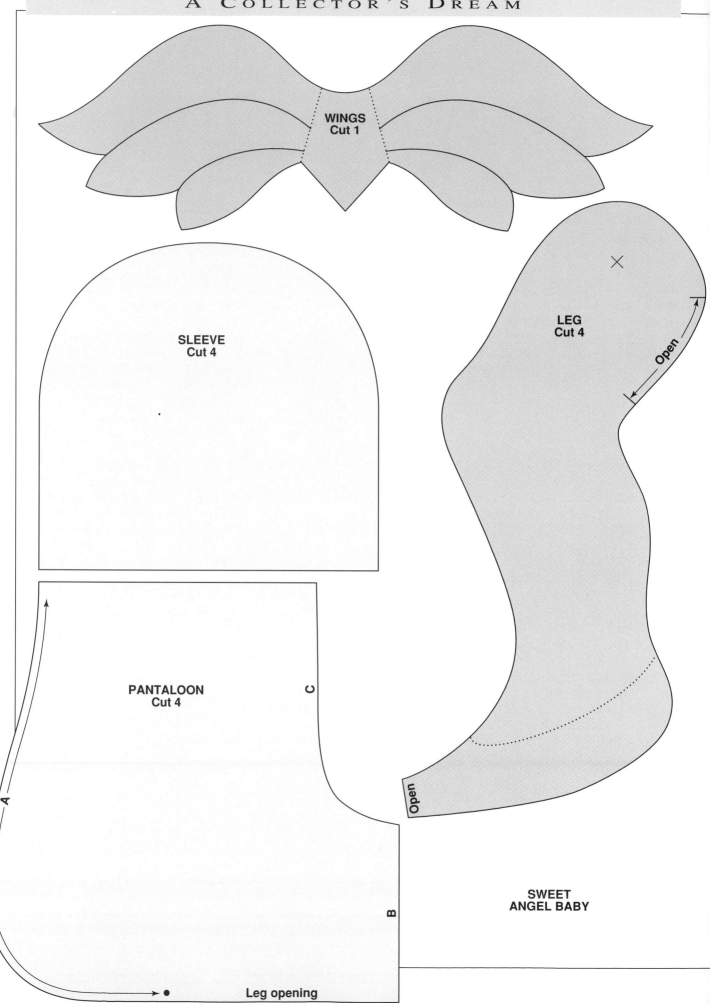

WINGS
Cut 1

SLEEVE
Cut 4

LEG
Cut 4

Open

Open

PANTALOON
Cut 4

C

A

B

Open

Leg opening

SWEET
ANGEL BABY

For pantaloon, sew two pieces together from top of side seam A to dot. Open piece out, turn under raw edge of each leg opening ¼ inch and hem. Fold piece back with right sides facing and stitch inner leg seam B. Repeat for remaining two pieces. Turn one piece right side out; slip it into the other piece aligning C seam edges. Sew seam, clip curve, and turn right side out. Turn under waistline raw edge ¼ inch; hem. Put pantaloon on doll; whipstitch waist to body, tucking as necessary to fit.

For skirt, sew trim strip to bottom long edge of skirt rectangle. Press seam toward trim. Sew short ends together. Turn under bottom raw edge ¼ inch; press. Fold trim in half to inside of skirt; blindstitch folded edge to seam line. Turn skirt right side out. Using a running stitch, gather waistline to fit doll's waist. Knot thread, adjust gathers, and whipstitch skirt waist to body.

For waistband, press under ¼ inch along one short end. Fold each long edge to the center, wrong sides facing, and press. Glue waistband around the skirt waist, overlapping in the back.

Stitch three beads down the center front of the bodice for buttons.

For arms, draw around the arm template two times onto doubled thickness of cotton knit; do not cut out. Sew along lines leaving open as indicated; cut out. Cut out arms ⅛ inch beyond the stitching. Turn arms right side out, stuff, and sew the openings closed. Backstitch along finger division lines using a doubled strand of sewing thread.

For sleeves, turn under ¼ inch along one long edge of each sleeve cuff and glue to secure. Turn under ¼ inch along one short end and glue. Wrap cuff, with the folded edge down, around wrist, placing the overlap at the inner arm.

Sew sleeves together in pairs, leaving straight bottom edge open; clip curve and turn right side out. Turn under ¼ inch along bottom raw edge; work running stitches around folded edge to gather the

sleeve. Pull sleeve over top of arm; pull gathering thread so sleeve fits snug around arm. Sleeve should overlap half of cuff. Knot thread. Cut tiny pearl strand length in half. Glue strand around top of each cuff. Sew arms to body as for legs, with buttons on outside of sleeves.

For wings, draw around pattern onto doubled thickness of interfacing; do not cut out. Using purple thread, sew along all lines. Cut out wings ⅛ inch beyond outline stitching. Paint each side with glitter paint, allowing first side to dry before painting the second. Fold the wings along the dotted lines; glue the center section to the doll's back.

TREETOP ANGEL

As shown on pages 114 and 117, angel is 14 inches tall.

MATERIALS
Tracing paper
10x26-inch piece of muslin
Embroidery hoop
Embroidery needle
Cotton embroidery floss: tan, brown, pink, green, rose, and white
Golden brown and ecru sewing threads
Powder blush
Small artist's brush
Polyester fiberfill
Two 14-inch-long pieces of dark blonde wool crepe hair
Hot glue gun
Glue sticks
½ yard of 72-inch-wide ecru netting
18x40-inch piece of ecru polyester chiffon
Gold tissue lamé as follows: one 6¼x40-inch rectangle, one 15½x40-inch rectangle, and two 2¾x2¾-inch squares
1 yard of ½-inch-wide gold metallic trim
6½ inches of ⅞-inch-wide gold metallic trim
Liquid seam sealant
Two sets of 5½-inch-long off-white neck hackle feathers
2 yards of 2⅞-inch-wide gold metallic wire-edge ribbon

INSTRUCTIONS
Trace patterns, *pages 126–127,* onto tracing paper and cut out. Cut arms and legs from muslin (seam allowances are included in pattern pieces). Use light box or bright window to trace body back and body front, including face, onto muslin; *do not* transfer dart markings. *Do not* cut out body pieces.

Sew all seams with right sides of fabric facing and use ¼-inch seam allowances unless otherwise indicated. Use small machine stitches to sew doll. Trim doll seams to ⅛ inch, clipping curves. To press the lamé, use cool dry iron and a press cloth. Treat the cut ends of metallic trims with seam sealant.

Embroider face using one strand of floss or thread throughout. Using embroidery floss, outline-stitch the eyebrows tan, the eyelids brown, and the nose curve pink. Satin-stitch pupils brown, irises green, and lips rose. Straight-stitch tiny white highlights in each eye and work two pink straight stitches for tip of nose. Straight-stitch eyelashes and outline irises using golden brown sewing thread. Brush cheeks with powder blush.

Cut out body front and back. Transfer darts to wrong sides. Sew darts. Sew front to back, leaving straight edge open. Turn right side out, stuff firmly, then turn under raw edges. Sew opening closed.

Sew arms and legs together in pairs, leaving tops open. Turn right side out, then stuff with fiberfill to the dots. With seams at sides, turn under raw edges of each limb; sew openings closed. Hand-sew arms to shoulders with thumbs pointing up. Hand-sew legs to body bottom with toes pointing out.

For hair, carefully unbraid and spread out each piece. Center and hot-glue one piece to back of head and remaining to top of head and sides of face.

For slip, fold and press netting to measure 9x36 inches. Sew short ends together for center back seam. Gather folded top edge to fit around waist; knot threads.

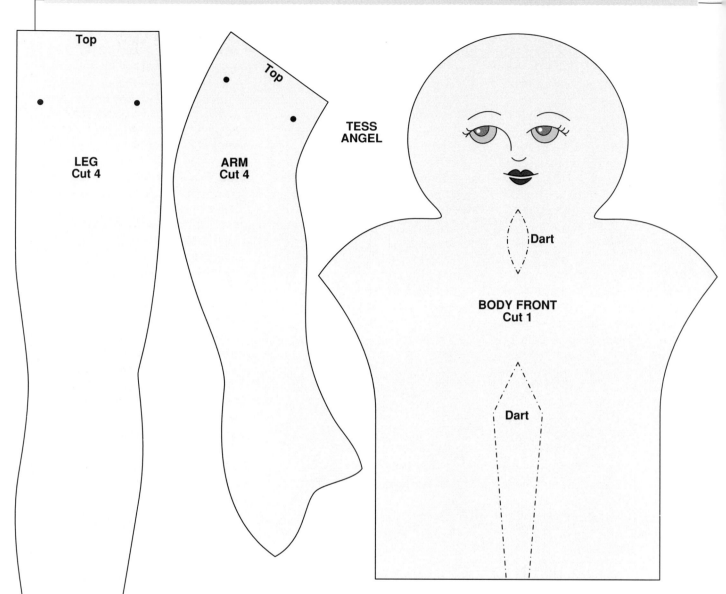

Top

**LEG
Cut 4**

Top

**ARM
Cut 4**

**TESS
ANGEL**

Dart

**BODY FRONT
Cut 1**

Dart

For gown, sew one long edge of 18x40-inch chiffon piece to one long edge of 6¼x40-inch lamé piece. Turn under ¼ inch along long raw edge of lamé; hem. Sew short ends together for center back seam. Fold lamé section to wrong side of gown for gown hem. Beginning at back seam, divide bottom edge into five equal sections; mark with a pencil. Then draw a 7½-inch-long vertical line at each mark; lines should be parallel to one another. Hand-gather the fabric along each line, pulling the gathers to measure 2 inches; knot threads. Cut five 4½-inch-long pieces of ½-inch-wide gold trim. Tack one end of the trim to top of gathers on right side of gown; loop trim around hem of gown and tack other end of trim to top of gathers on wrong side of gown.

Sew short ends of 15½x40-inch lamé rectangle for center back seam of the underskirt. Turn under 1¾ inches twice along one long edge for hem; sew in place.

Sew together top edge of chiffon gown and lamé underskirt, with right side of gown facing wrong side of underskirt. Press seam toward lamé. Turn to right side and press fold in chiffon ¼ inch above seam for gown top edge.

Mark 1-inch-long armhole lines (perpendicular to top edge), placing each line 10 inches from center back seam. Sew around armhole

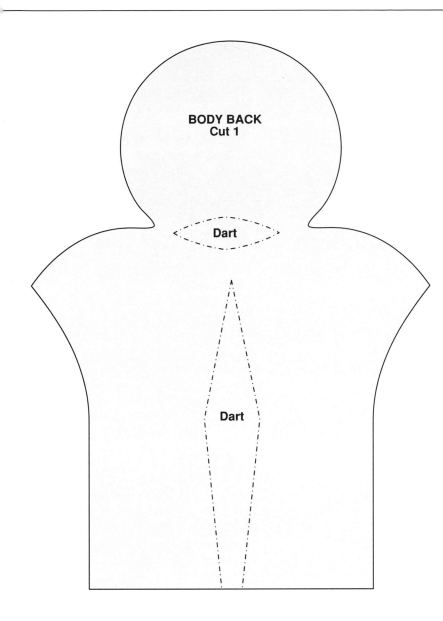

BODY BACK
Cut 1

Dart

Dart

FROSTY, NO-SEW SNOW FAMILY

As shown on pages 114 and 118, snowman is 10 inches tall, snow lady is 8½ inches tall, and snow junior is 7 inches tall.

MATERIALS

Two 5-inch-diameter plastic-foam balls
Two 2- or 2½-inch-diameter jar lids
Hot-glue gun
Glue sticks
Two 4-inch-diameter plastic-foam balls (cut one of the balls in half)
1½-inch-diameter jar lid
18-gauge floral wire
Two 2½-inch-diameter plastic-foam balls (cut one of the balls in half)
Two 3-inch-diameter plastic-foam balls
Four 1½-inch-diameter plastic-foam balls
Eight 2-inch-diameter plastic-foam balls
Three jars of Duncan Snow Accents texturing material
Orange bakable modeling clay
Crafts knife; crafts glue
Six 5-millimeter black half-round beads
Tracing paper
6x8-inch piece of dark blue polar fleece (snowman hat and snow lady mittens)
Three 1-inch-diameter light blue pom poms (snowman hat and snow junior earmuff)
8x18-inch piece of teal polar fleece (snow lady hat, snowman mittens, and snow junior scarf)
10x19-inch piece of multicolor polar fleece (snow lady cape and snowman scarf)
4x4-inch piece of light blue polar fleece (snow junior mittens)
White string
2x19-inch piece of bright pink polar fleece (snow lady scarf)
Yellow terry cloth pipe cleaner (snow junior earmuff)
11 assorted plastic buttons
Small bits of Christmas greenery or miniature pinecones
Iridescent spray glitter

lines using small machine stitches. Cut armhole lines, press raw edges under, and edgestitch.

Sew two rows of gathering stitches along doubled (¼-inch-wide) chiffon layer at top front and back edges. Sew one row of gathering stitches for waist 1⅜ inches down from top. Put gown on doll. Pull up gathers to fit across bodice front and back as shown in photograph, *page 117,* and knot threads. Repeat for waist. Wrap ½-inch-wide gold trim tightly around waist; sew edges together at center back. Hand sew ½-inch-wide gold trim to bodice top edge in one piece, wrapping trim around shoulders. Sew edges together at center back.

For halo, sew together the ends of ⅞-inch-wide trim to form a circle; sew to the head with the seam at the back.

For wings, sew opposite sides of lamé squares together to make a tube. Turn right side out; press raw edges to inside. Insert base of one feather set into each open end; topstitch through all layers to secure feathers. Hand gather through center of lamé midsection from bottom to top; pull up gathers and knot thread. Hand tack gathered feathers to back of doll.

Shape long wide gold ribbon into flowing curves. Referring to photograph, gather ribbon at hands and tack to secure. Shape ribbon.

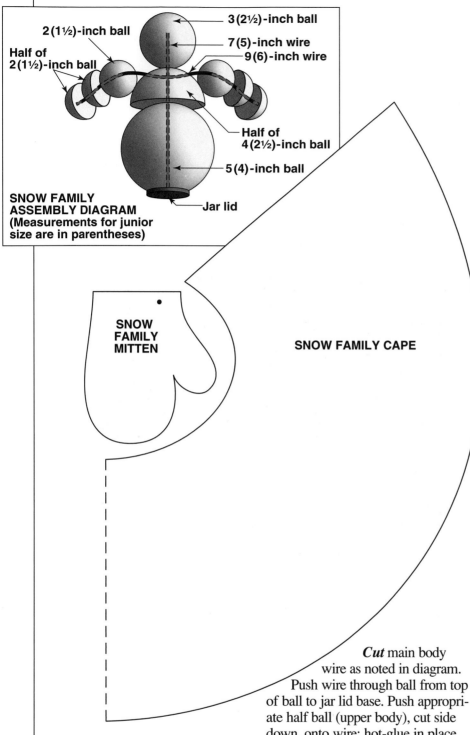

SNOW FAMILY ASSEMBLY DIAGRAM
(Measurements for junior size are in parentheses)

- 2 (1½)-inch ball
- 3 (2½)-inch ball
- 7 (5)-inch wire
- 9 (6)-inch wire
- Half of 2 (1½)-inch ball
- Half of 4 (2½)-inch ball
- 5 (4)-inch ball
- Jar lid

SNOW FAMILY MITTEN

SNOW FAMILY CAPE

INSTRUCTIONS

Follow diagram, *above,* while assembling figures. Measurements on diagram are for snowman and snow lady; measurements in parentheses are for snow junior.

Wedge a large jar lid into a 5-inch plastic-foam ball for base of snowman; hot-glue in place. Repeat for base of snow lady. Assemble snow junior base in same manner, except use small jar lid and a 4-inch ball.

Cut main body wire as noted in diagram. Push wire through ball from top of ball to jar lid base. Push appropriate half ball (upper body), cut side down, onto wire; hot-glue in place. Hot-glue head ball onto wire.

Insert and center arm wire horizontally through upper body, pushing wire through area closer to back. Push one arm ball onto each end of wire; slide up to body. Cut two small arm balls in half. Slide one half-ball onto each side as shown in diagram. Shape remaining half balls each by squeezing opposite sides to make longer and more narrow for hands. Slide hands onto wires off-center, so

they appear to curve toward body front. Position arms as desired and hot-glue to secure in place. Smooth out arms by pressing firmly with fingers. Press around torso to smooth waistline. Using fingers, apply Snow Accents over snow figures.

For carrot noses, knead orange clay until pliable. Roll three ⅜-inch-diameter balls. Shape each ball into a ⅞-inch-long carrot. Rotating carrot, score carrot-like ridges using a crafts knife. Bake carrots in 225° oven for 15 minutes; let cool. Push wide end of carrot into center of each face; hot-glue in place.

Glue bead eyes to heads, placing eyes about ¼ inch above carrot nose.

For snowman hat, cut a 4x6-inch rectangle from the dark blue fleece. Fold the rectangle in half, matching 4-inch-long edges. Glue one of the doubled 3-inch-long sides together for the back seam; turn to right side. Position hat on snowman's head and hot-glue to secure. Fold front edge back ½ inch for brim; hot-glue in place. Tuck and glue hat around neck. Hot-glue pom pom to tip.

For snow lady hat, cut a 5x6-inch rectangle from teal fleece. Hot-glue center 3 inches on one 6-inch edge around lower head back. Pull each of two back corner points to center of back edge, shaping back of hat. Fold front long edge back ½ inch for brim; hot-glue around face. Glue hat to head around bottom side edges.

For snow lady cape, trace pattern, *left,* onto tracing paper; cut out. Cut cape from multicolor fleece. Drape over shoulders and glue to secure.

For mittens, trace pattern, *left,* onto tracing paper and cut out. Cut six mittens, two for each snow figure, from fleece colors as noted in materials list. Knot end of 7-inch-long string through tiny hole in tip of each mitten. Cut ¼x2-inch strip of contrasting color polar fleece for each mitten. Glue strip around top edge of mitten for trim, covering string knot; cut away excess. Tie end of mitten string around each hand.

For scarves, cut two 1¼x19-inch strips: one from bright pink fleece for snow lady; the other from multicolor fleece for snowman. Cut a 1¼x15-inch strip from teal fleece for snow junior. Fringe ends. Style scarves around necks; glue to secure.

For snow junior's earmuff, cut pipe cleaner to 9 inches. Fold in half and glue ends to head sides. Hot-glue pom-poms over ends of pipe cleaner.

Glue one or two colored buttons to each scarf as shown in photograph, *page 118.* Glue one button to upper body of snow lady, two buttons down front of snow junior, and three buttons down front of snowman. Glue small bits of Christmas greenery, miniature pinecones, and/or small buttons to hat brims.

Spray figures with glitter. Wipe glitter from eyes before it dries.

HERBAL SNOWMAN

As shown on page 119, snowman measures 12 inches tall.

MATERIALS

Four tea bags
15x12-inch piece of muslin
Tracing paper
Water-erasable fabric marker
6x12-inch piece of dark red print
Sewing thread: ecru and dark red
Polyester fiberfill
13-inch-long cinnamon stick
Crafts glue; hot-glue gun; glue sticks
Black permanent artist's pen, size 03
Orange bakable modeling clay
Crafts knife
Kite string
Springerii (air fern) for carrot tops
72 inches of 18-gauge dark annealed
    stovepipe wire
⅜-inch-diameter dowel, 5 inches long
Nine ½-inch-diameter brown buttons
1⅛x20-inch strip of wool (scarf)
Small package of red potpourri
Six small bay leaves
Black buttonhole thread
Three ¾-inch-diameter pinecones
One star-shaped anise seed
3-inch-diameter grapevine wreath
Small sprigs of blue lavendula, red
    pepper berries, black spruce, blue
    delphinium, wheat, and eucalyptus
Two miniature pinecones
7-inch-tall miniature broom

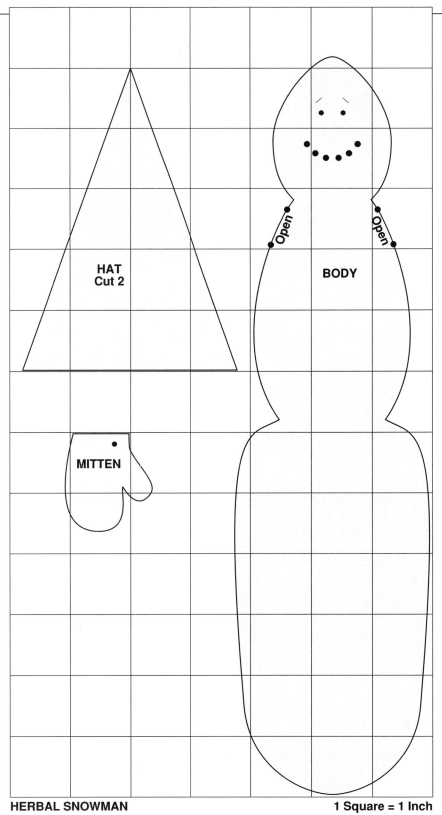

HAT
Cut 2

BODY

Open

Open

MITTEN

HERBAL SNOWMAN

1 Square = 1 Inch

INSTRUCTIONS

To tea-dye muslin, prepare a strong tea solution by steeping tea bags in 3 cups of hot water. Soak fabric in tea until it is slightly darker than desired color. Squeeze out excess liquid and place on a flat surface to dry. When dry, press on medium heat.

Enlarge pattern, *above,* and trace onto tracing paper; cut out. Use fabric marker to draw around body pattern onto a double thickness of muslin (transfer facial features, also) and around mitten pattern two times on a double thickness of dark red print; *do not* cut out. Cut hat pieces from remaining dark red print.

Sew around body outline, leaving open as marked on pattern. Cut out body ¼ inch beyond stitching; clip curves. Cut 1¼-inch-long slit in neck back and turn body right side out. Stuff head with fiberfill. Insert cinnamon stick through arm holes and stuff remainder of body. Whipstitch neck opening closed. Use a small amount of crafts glue to secure cinnamon stick near bottom of each arm hole. Draw face in place using permanent pen.

For carrot nose, roll orange clay into ¼-inch-diameter ball. Shape into a ¾-inch-long carrot. Rotating carrot, score carrot-like ridges with a crafts knife. Cut the carrot top flat for ease in attaching to body.

Make five more carrots from ⅜-inch-diameter balls of clay (leave carrot tops rounded); make hole with needle in each carrot top to receive greenery stem. Pierce another hole through center of each carrot so they can be strung together after baking.

Bake carrots in 225° oven for 10 minutes; allow to cool. Glue carrot nose to face. String the remaining carrots onto 6 inches of kite string, knotting string between carrots. Glue small bit of Springerii into top of each carrot. Set strung carrots aside.

Wrap wire around dowel, beginning 3½ inches from end of wire; referring to photograph, *page 119,* create a coil about 3 inches long. Thread a button onto the wire. Continue wrapping the wire and threading buttons; end with a 3-inch coil. Remove the wire from dowel. Twist the straight ends around the cinnamon-stick arms.

Fringe ends of wool scarf. Wrap around snowman's neck, drape over cinnamon stick, and glue to secure.

Sew long sides of hat pieces together using ¼-inch seams; turn right side out. Glue to head; tack point to right side of head.

For mittens, stitch along curved outlines drawn on fabric, leaving bottoms unstitched. Cut out ⅛ inch beyond sewing lines. Clip curves and

turn right side out. Knot one end of 5-inch length of string through dots on each mitten pair. Set aside.

String 6 inches of black buttonhole thread with red potpourri pieces, pinecones, two buttons, and bay leaves. Tie each end of thread onto cinnamon-stick arms 2 inches from body so strand drapes in front.

Sew three buttons down lower front section of snowman. Hot-glue anise seed pod to right side of waist.

Hot-glue pepperberries and small pinecones to front of miniature broom. Glue string to top of handle for hanging. Knot a length of buttonhole thread to the wreath, blue lavendula, black spruce, blue delphinium, wheat, and eucalyptus for hanging. Hang shapes from cinnamon-stick arms, referring to the photograph, *page 119,* for placement.

PRIMITIVE SANTA

As shown on pages 115 and 120, Santa is 22 inches tall.

MATERIALS

Tracing paper
¾ yard of unbleached muslin
Dressmaker's carbon paper
Plastic wrap
Paint brush
Apple Barrel acrylic paints: No. 20546 red, No. 20521 nutmeg brown, No. 20504 black, No. 20575 sandstone, and No. 20585 satin cream
½- and 1-inch-wide flat artists' brushes
Small natural sponge
Black permanent fine-tip marker
Stencil brush
16 tea bags
Polyester fiberfill
Large darning needle; cotton string
Black embroidery floss
One ½-inch-diameter white button
Two ¾-inch-diameter black buttons

INSTRUCTIONS

Enlarge pattern, *opposite,* onto tracing paper and cut out (pattern pieces include seam allowances). Transfer body and leg outlines and all details onto muslin using dressmaker's carbon paper.

Sew all fabric pieces together *with wrong sides of fabric facing,* using ¼-inch seam allowances. Sew the body pieces together, leaving the bottom straight edge open. Sew the legs together in pairs, leaving the tops open.

Position plastic wrap inside the body and the legs to prevent paint on one side from bleeding through to the other. Using a paint brush, paint the hat, suit, and legs red. Paint the mittens nutmeg brown and the boots black. Using the sponge, paint the beard, mustache, hat fur, and the back of Santa's neck sandstone. When the paint on the fur and beard are dry, lightly sponge over these areas with satin cream. Outline the nose using the permanent black marker. Blush Santa's cheeks with red using the stencil brush. Allow all of the pieces to dry.

Prepare a strong tea solution by steeping 16 tea bags in ½ gallon hot water; remove the bags. Soak the body and legs in the solution until they are slightly darker than the desired shade. Squeeze out excess tea and allow the pieces to dry.

Stuff legs to the knee with polyester fiberfill. Hold each leg so the front and back seams match; sew across each leg at the knee as indicated on the pattern, using a darning needle threaded with cotton string and working small running stitches. Stuff legs to the top and pin closed. Then stuff the body and pin the bottom edge closed.

Pin the leg tops to the body, lapping them over the bottom edge of the body. Using cotton string and small running stitches, sew the body opening closed, catching the legs in the seam.

To detail Santa, work French-knot eyes using three plies of black embroidery floss. With cotton string, attach the white button to the hat and the black buttons to the suit front at Xs. To attach buttons, sew down through one hole in the button, in and out of the fabric, and then up through the other button hole; knot the string on the front of the button.

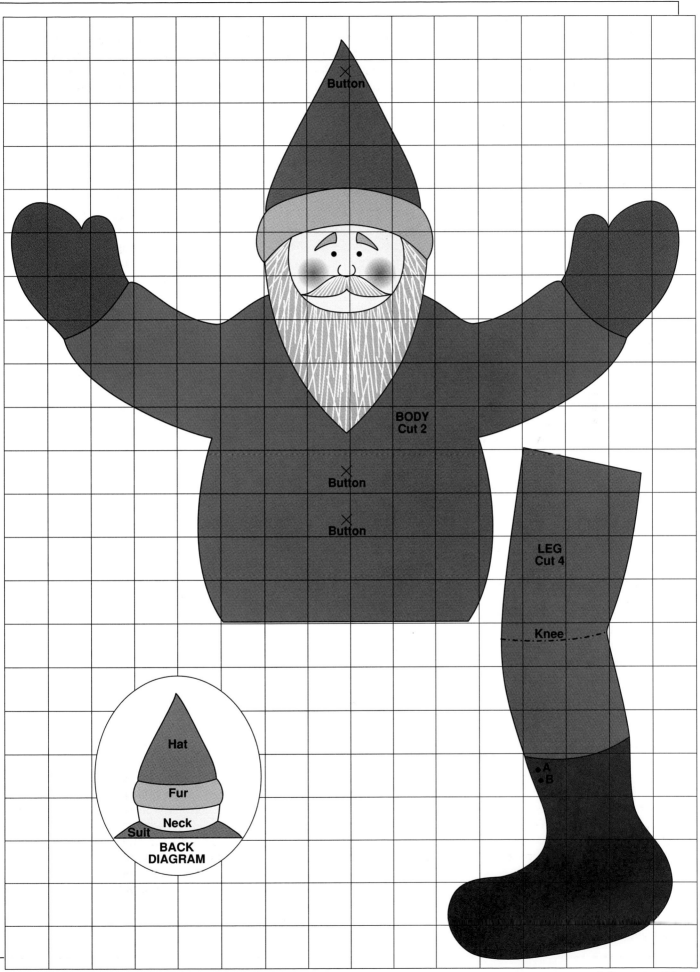

Button

Button

BODY
Cut 2

Button

LEG
Cut 4

Knee

•A
•B

Hat

Fur

Neck

Suit

BACK
DIAGRAM

PRIMITIVE SANTA

1 Square = 1 Inch

For boot ties, push needle threaded with 10 inches of string into point A and out at point B on one side, and into point B and out point A on the other side of the boot. Tie string into a bow and trim the ends.

Sew random long stitches with cotton string to detail the eyebrows, mustache, and beard as indicated on the pattern.

LOVABLE ELF SANTA

As shown on pages 114 and 121, seated Santa is 14 inches tall.

MATERIALS

Fabric measurements are for 45-inch-wide fabric.

Tracing paper

¼ yard of peach felt

¼ yard of unbleached muslin

¼ yard of black-and-red check polar fleece (hat and jacket)

7x20-inch piece of ivory short nap fur or fleece (jacket sleeves and trim)

¼ yard of green knit fabric (pants and scarf)

Brown paper

Sewing threads to match fabric, including black

Fabric glue

Polyester fiberfill

Two round-headed brass fasteners

Acrylic paints: black, red, and yellow

Small flat artist's brush

Long soft-sculpture needle

Brown eye shadow

¼ yard of black-and-red mini-check fabric (lower leg)

Dental floss

Ten 10-millimeter wood beads

⅔ yard of 1-inch-wide decorative woven trim

White wool roving

⅞-inch-diameter jingle bell

Tiny seed pods or pinecones

Purchased dark red doll boots, with the soles approximately 2¾ inches long

6x6x12-inch doll chair

Cream paper

Gold and black pens

INSTRUCTIONS

Trace only the clothing, body, head back, and forehead pieces on *pages 133, 135,* and *136* onto tracing paper; cut out.

Cut head back and forehead from peach felt, body from muslin, hat and jacket from polar fleece, and pants from green knit. In addition, cut two 4½x7-inch sleeve rectangles and one 2x20-inch jacket trim strip from fur and a 4x20-inch scarf rectangle from green knit.

Transfer the head front profile, *page 133,* and the upper arm, lower arm, upper leg, lower leg, and toe and heel guide patterns, *page 134,* onto brown paper to make templates; cut out.

Patterns include the necessary seam allowances. Sew all clothing seams with right sides of fabric facing and use ¼-inch seam allowances, unless otherwise indicated. Follow the individual instructions closely for stitching the body and head pieces.

For the head, draw around head front profile template onto double thickness of felt; do not cut out. Stitch center front seam along drawn line. Cut out head ⅛ inch away from stitching and along drawn lines around perimeter. Turn head front right side out. Dot inside of nose with glue and stuff with small piece of fiberfill. Set the head aside.

Paint brass fasteners black. When dry, push the fasteners into face for eyes. Bend the prongs to hold the fasteners in place.

Turn under ¼ inch along inner curve of forehead and glue to secure. Position forehead over top of face with folded edge along dotted line (refer to pattern piece). The forehead piece should cover the top one-fourth of the eye, creating eyelids.

Run a thin line of glue along the center front seam on the face behind the forehead area only; press forehead to the face. To shape the eyelids, work running stitches using pale peach sewing thread along the dotted line over each eye.

Sew the head front to the back using a ⅛-inch seam allowance; leave open at bottom as indicated for turning. Turn head right side out and stuff with fiberfill, adding extra fiberfill to cheeks. Sew opening closed.

Using the soft-sculpture needle and a single strand of black sewing thread, insert needle from the back of the head and out near the corner of one eye. Referring to the face diagram, *page 133,* work straight stitches around each eye. For the mouth, work long straight stitches as shown in diagram using a double strand of black thread. Define the bridge of the nose by stitching back and forth several times between the inner corners of the eyes using pale peach thread. Blush cheeks using thinned red paint. Rub brown eye shadow over the eyelids.

For the body, sew the front to the back, leaving the neck edge open. Turn body right side out and stuff firmly, stopping ½ inch from top. Turn under ¼ inch along opening; sew opening closed.

For arms and legs, draw twice around upper arm and upper leg template onto double thickness of muslin, twice around lower arm template onto double thickness of peach felt, and twice around lower leg template onto black-and-red mini-check fabric; *do not* cut out. Stitch along drawn lines leaving open as indicated on pattern pieces. Cut out each piece ⅛ inch beyond stitching and turn all shapes right side out, except lower legs. Stuff upper arm, lower arm, and upper leg, then sew openings closed. Backstitch along finger division (dot-and-dash) lines on lower arm.

Flatten each foot part of lower leg, wrong side out, with top and bottom seams matching. Place toe template on toe edge of flattened foot. Draw around template curve reversing template for opposite foot. Stitch along drawn line. Cut out each foot ⅛ inch away from stitching. For each heel, match center back and bottom seams and flatten, forming a triangular configuration. Place heel template on triangle ½ inch down from point. Draw around heel curve, stitch, and cut as for toe. Turn lower legs right side

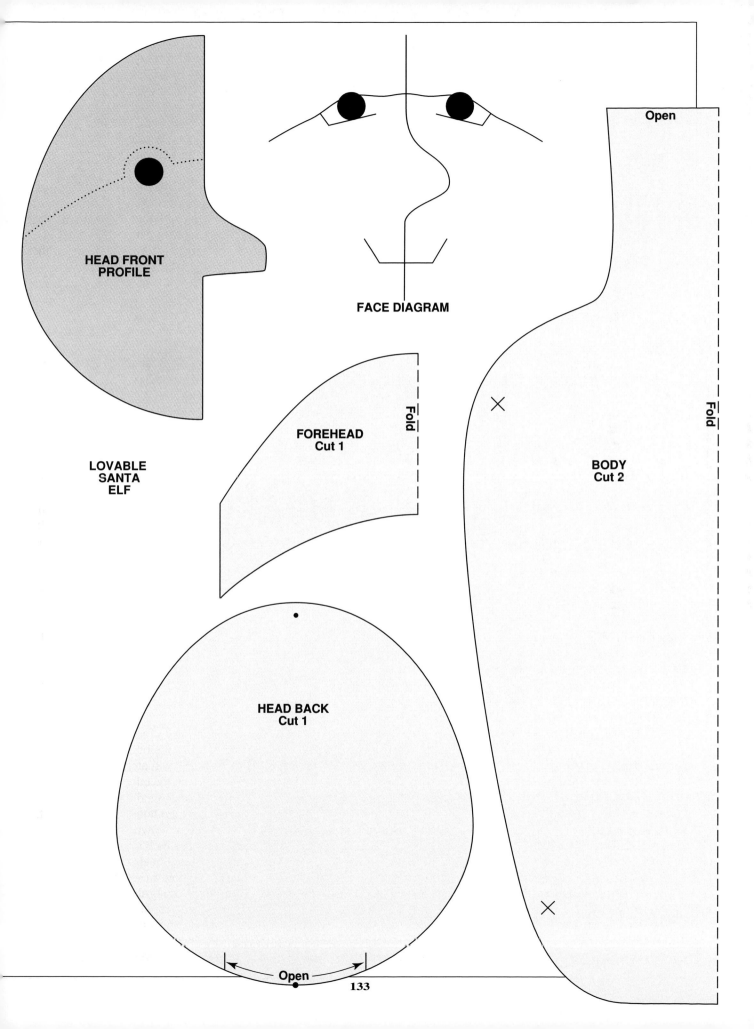

HEAD FRONT
PROFILE

FACE DIAGRAM

LOVABLE
SANTA
ELF

FOREHEAD
Cut 1

Fold

BODY
Cut 2

Fold

Open

HEAD BACK
Cut 1

Open

133

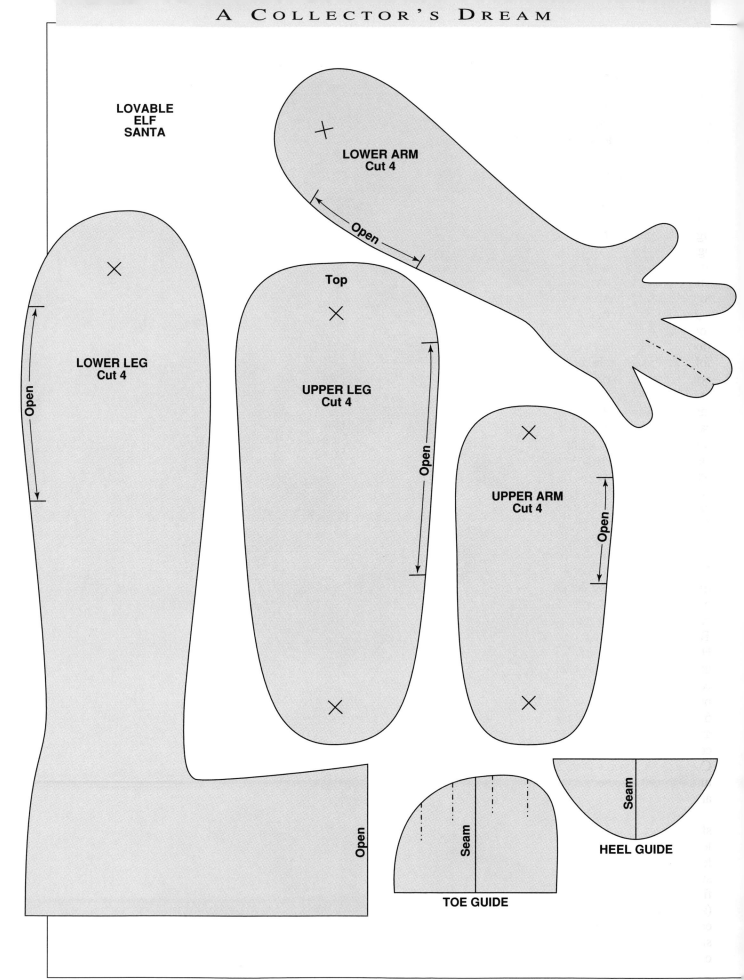

LOVABLE
ELF
SANTA

LOWER ARM
Cut 4

Open

LOWER LEG
Cut 4

Open

Top

UPPER LEG
Cut 4

Open

UPPER ARM
Cut 4

Open

Open

Seam

TOE GUIDE

Seam

HEEL GUIDE

out and stuff. Sew openings closed. Using black thread, backstitch toe divisions as shown on toe template.

Overlap each lower arm over end of one upper arm, matching Xs. Using needle threaded with double strand of dental floss, push needle through overlapped area at X. Slide bead onto needle and push needle back through to other side. Slide another bead onto needle, pull floss tight, and push it through arm once again. Sew back and forth through arm and beads four more times and knot floss. Whipstitch tops of arms to body at shoulders, matching Xs.

Join lower legs to upper legs as for arms. Using needle and dental floss, sew jointed legs to body as follows: Push needle through lower body from left to right, entering and exiting at Xs. Next, push needle through X at top of jointed leg in same manner. Slide bead onto the needle and push back through leg and body. Push needle through remaining jointed leg at X. Slide another bead onto needle and push back through body. Sew back and forth through body, legs, and beads several times and knot floss.

For pants, sew inseam from A to B on each piece. Turn one piece right side out; slip leg into other pant leg, matching seams. Sew pieces together along curved seam. Turn right side out; put on Santa. Hand-sew pants to Santa's waist, gathering as necessary. Gather each pant leg ⅛ inch from the bottom edge to fit leg. Glue 6 inches of embroidered trim around the gathered edge, covering gathering stitches. Cut away the excess trim, turn under the raw edge, and glue in place.

For jacket, fold each sleeve rectangle in half lengthwise. Sew the long edges together, stopping 2 inches from one end (sleeve top). Turn each sleeve right side out and slide onto arm with

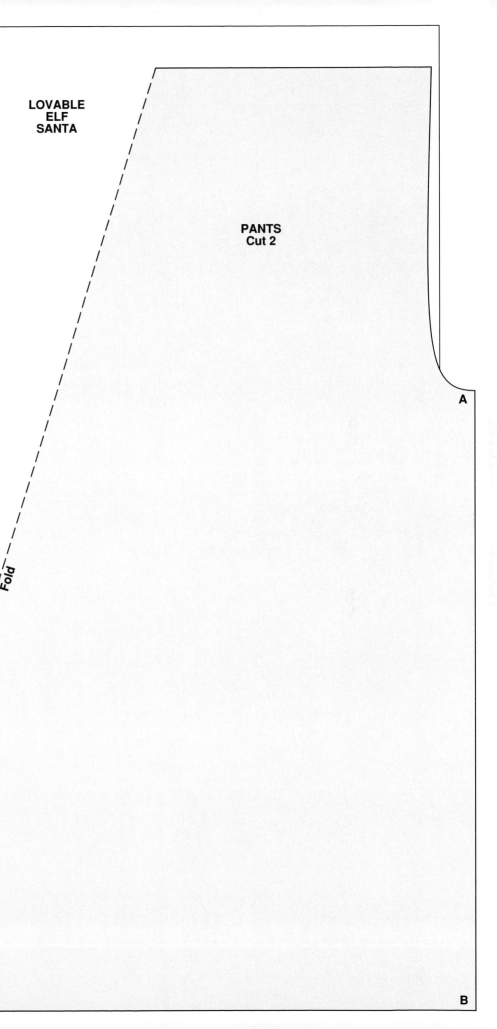

LOVABLE
ELF
SANTA

PANTS
Cut 2

Fold

A

B

seam along underarm. Pull sleeve top over shoulder and around arm; whipstitch to body.

Cut jacket from A to B on dashed line to make neck opening. Sew side seams from bottom to dot and turn jacket right side out. Join short ends of 2x20-inch fur strip. Sew one long edge to bottom edge of jacket. Turn fur to inside and whipstitch raw edge to seam. Put the jacket on Santa, pulling arms through side openings. Turn under ¼ inch along side opening edges and glue to sleeves at shoulders and underarms. Glue embroidered trim around each sleeve bottom. Fringe short ends of scarf; set scarf aside.

For head and beard, position head at top of neck, tipped slightly to figure's right side. Hand-sew the head in place. Dab glue under chin, around sides of face, and at back of neck. Pull out small tufts of wool roving and glue three or four tufts under chin and along sides of face.

Glue larger tuft to head back, covering neck. Glue small bits of wool over eyes for the eyebrows. Twist a tuft of wool; glue under nose for mustache.

For hat, sew front to back, leaving bottom open. Stuff hat lightly; sew jingle bell to point. Position the hat on the head and slip-stitch in place. Glue the tiny seed pods or pinecones around front bottom edge.

For list, cut 3x15-inch strip of brown paper. Write names on paper to make Santa's list.

Tie scarf around neck, put boots on feet, and set Santa in chair.

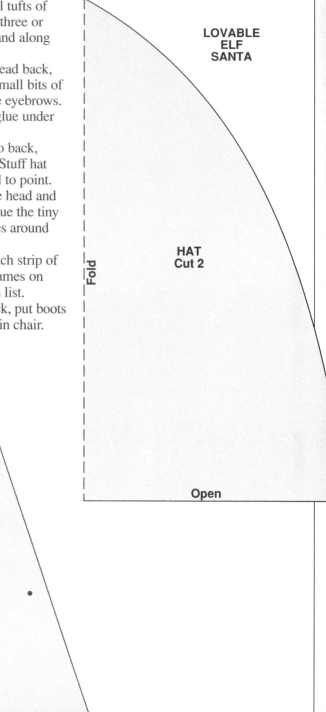

LOVABLE
ELF
SANTA

Fold

HAT
Cut 2

Open

A

B

Fold

Fold

JACKET
FRONT / BACK
Cut 1

The Giving Tree

ᴸike turning pages in a family photo album, decorating the Christmas tree fills our hearts with warm and joyous memories. As each ornament is looped over a branch, it brings with it visions of Christmases past, all the while imparting the spirit of this most loving and giving season. The tree truly is the heart of our holiday decorating. In its honor, we offer these glorious trims and gift wraps.

PHOTOGRAPHER: HOPKINS ASSOCIATES

A Tree of Gifts

This year, spread the giving spirit to the branches of your Christmas tree. For a special gift tree, have all the members of your family craft new trims. Then, when friends and houseguests come for holiday visits, ask them to pick a favorite gift from the tree to take home as a special remembrance. Turn the next few pages for a closer look at the dozen-plus ideas to make and give shown here.

PHOTOGRAPHER: SCOTT LITTLE

With ornamental treasures this delightful and varied, you'll find it easy to pick ones that suit just about every member of your family. Some are as quick and fun to do as tying a pretty bow, while others require crafting skills, such as cross-stitching, painting, tatting, and crocheting. Then, to round out your Christmas tree decor, piece clever patchwork wreaths and sew them into the quilted heirloom tree skirt and matching wall hanging, below.

QUILTED CHRISTMAS-WREATH TREE SKIRT AND WALL HANGING

*D*on the walls with quilted treasures—the floor around the tree, too—with this coordinating duo of red-and-green patchwork. An ingenious pattern of seasonal wreaths forms a wall hanging when the block is pieced straight and set with sashing strips. Sewn on the diagonal, the wreath pattern encircles the tree, forming an eight-point star in the skirt's center. Both are trimmed with fa-la-la-la-lots of beads and tinkling bells. Instructions begin on page 146.

DESIGNER: PHYLLIS DOBBS ● PHOTOGRAPHER: SCOTT LITTLE

JACK-IN-THE-BOX ORNAMENT

*I*t may be pint-sized, but this Jack-in-the-box trim packs plenty of big-time crafting fun. Made from snippets of plastic canvas, Aida cloth, and floss, it's covered from top to bottom in cross-stitches. Beads, braid, and pom-pom accents make this one a real treasure. Instructions are on page 149.

DESIGNER: LOIS WINSTON ● PHOTOGRAPHER: SCOTT LITTLE

ROLY-POLY SANTA

*S*anta's image is written on our hearts and captured forever in this jolly tree trim. About 6 inches tall, the pine cutout has all the right details painted in place. Instructions are on page 151 and the pattern is on page 152.

DESIGNER: SUSAN CAGE-KNOCH
PHOTOGRAPHER: SCOTT LITTLE

THE CHRISTMAS ROSE

*I*f you could purchase ribbons in seed packets and sow them on your Christmas tree, in minutes, they would bloom into fragrant roses all over the branches. The trick to these floral beauties? It's wire-edge ribbon that has been shaped and gathered with simple hand-taken stitches. Instructions are on page 151.

DESIGNER: MARGARET SINDELAR
PHOTOGRAPHER: SCOTT LITTLE

GOOD-DOG TREAT

*D*ecorate purchased dog biscuits with red ribbon bows. Then place them in a bowlful near the tree so you can treat every good dog that comes by with his tail a-waggin'.

PHOTOGRAPHER: SCOTT LITTLE

EMBROIDERED DOILY ORNAMENT

*R*eady to thrill? Here's a pretty frill that whips up in a jiffy with purchased doilies and festive ribbon embroidery. Instructions begin on page 152.

DESIGNER: PHYLLIS DOBBS ● PHOTOGRAPHER: SCOTT LITTLE

TATTED JINGLE FLAKE

*T*he perfect symmetry of a frosty snowflake is reflected in this tatted beauty. Tiny bells at the snowtips and center give a gentle jingle when holiday visitors walk by. Instructions, page 153.

DESIGNER: MARY H. McCARTHY
PHOTOGRAPHER: SCOTT LITTLE

CRYSTAL-CLEAR HOBBY ORNAMENTS

*O*ne suits a golfer to a tee, the other catches a fisherman's eye. It's clear, these ornamental possibilities are as endless as your imagination. Just pick the theme, then fill purchased hollow plastic shapes with tiny trinkets for loads of holiday fun and surprises.

PHOTOGRAPHER: SCOTT LITTLE

SUGAR-SWEET GARLAND TREAT

*F*or this garland, wrapped candies slide down a sheer ribbon tubing, stopping when bright bows tie them off into little pockets. Instructions, page 154.

DESIGNER: MARGARET SINDELAR
PHOTOGRAPHER: SCOTT LITTLE

BOOKMARK TRIO

*R*eady to mark the branches of your Christmas tree, these bookish ornamentals can do double-duty as the real thing, too. Cross-stitch the designs on 14-count Aida banding, trim with lace, and finish into bookmark shapes yourself. Instructions and patterns are on pages 154–155.

DESIGNER: ALICE OKON ● PHOTOGRAPHER: SCOTT LITTLE

RIBBON BOW

*F*estive picot and plaid ribbons can always perform as a gift bow or hair bow. But here they steal the show in the role of holiday ornaments. We've shown hair bows made with purchased barrette hardware designed for gathering ribbon.

PHOTOGRAPHER: SCOTT LITTLE

TASSELED SNOW LACE

*G*et ready, get set, snow! With a crochet trio this easy, pristine snowflakes fall in a flurry from your fingertips to dance on the tree. Starched to keep their shape, they become dimensional when you tack three together with a tassel. Instructions, page 154.

DESIGNER: HELENE RUSH
PHOTOGRAPHER: SCOTT LITTLE

Ok, so you can't judge a book—or a gift—by its cover. But with spiffy wrappings like these, why bother? The trims are sweet presents all by themselves! Try one or all five of these fabulous ideas for dressing up the extra-special packages on your holiday list.

GILDED CHRISTMAS CORSAGE

Nuts and pinecone rosettes burst into bloom when you plant them on a sunny package. Purchase flower-like pinecones at craft and florist supply stores or gather ones from your own backyard for the blossoms. Let Brazil nuts and pecans serve as leaves. Then spray the shapes with gold paint. When they're dry, hot-glue them directly to your package. Or, glue them to a round of cardboard and attach a gold hanging loop or a pin-back for an ornamental that can be enjoyed long after the gift is unwrapped.

DESIGNER: CAROL FIELD DAHLSTROM ● PHOTOGRAPHER: HOPKINS ASSOCIATES

HOLIDAY DRESS-UP

This year, let your Christmas packages play dress-up. Choose a pretty wrapping paper for the "blouse" and add a Battenburg doily "collar" in the center. Next, fashion a satin "bow-tie." Then loop a tassel over the bow-tie and hot-glue a brass charm atop its knot for the "brooch." You can hot-glue all of the components in place, but to preserve extra-special and heirloom pieces, use adhesive tape, safety pins, or pretty thread ties whenever possible.

DESIGNER: CAROL FIELD DAHLSTROM
PHOTOGRAPHER: HOPKINS ASSOCIATES

KID'S CRAYON RAIN-"BOW"

Creating this lighthearted package trim is child's play. Simply spin a color wheel of crayons around a small sharpener placed in the center of a wrapped present, and the fun-and-games begin. A dab here and there of hot glue makes for quick-as-a-wink assembly. It allows for easy removal and reuse of the sharpener and crayons, too.

DESIGNER: CAROL FIELD DAHLSTROM
PHOTOGRAPHER: HOPKINS ASSOCIATES

MAKING A BOW

1. Form four 6-inch coils using a 60-inch length of ribbon, allowing 6 inches for tails on opposite sides.

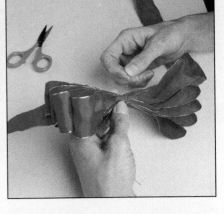

2. Pinch ribbon in the center of the coils, then wrap it tightly with a piece of thin-gauge wire.

3. Make a 2-inch-diameter loop for the center "knot." Wire knot to the center of the bow.

4. Wire bow to a package tied with matching ribbon. Shape loops to create a full bow. Trim ribbon tails.

FUN-BURST FANTASY

*W*atch your kids smile when they see this festival of balloons, candy, and ribbon curls. To start the fun, begin by wrapping two strands of curling ribbon around a brightly wrapped package.

Use additional strands of curling ribbon to secure five balloons to the stick of a large lollipop. With tube frosting, write your child's name on the lollipop, then tie it to package.

Curl all of the ribbon ends, adding more ribbon to fill out the arrangement, as necessary.

DESIGNER: CAROL FIELD DAHLSTROM
PHOTOGRAPHER: HOPKINS ASSOCIATES

BEADED, BEJEWELED, AND BEDAZZLING

*H*ere's a gem of an idea. Wrap a corner of your present with strands of glittery Christmas garland, then tie them all up with a brooch "bow." If you like, accessorize the gift tag, too. Pierce it with one earring (or a pair), a pretty tie tack, or an antique hat pin, or glue on a sparkling button.

DESIGNER: CAROL FIELD DAHLSTROM
PHOTOGRAPHER: HOPKINS ASSOCIATES

QUILTED CHRISTMAS-WREATH TREE SKIRT AND WALL HANGING

As shown on pages 138–139 and 140, tree skirt is 45 inches in diameter and wall hanging measures 32x41 inches.

MATERIALS

For tree skirt and wall hanging

Fabric yardages are for 45-inch-wide fabrics

Tracing paper

Cardboard or template plastic

Erasable fabric marker

Quilt batting; clear nylon sewing thread

For tree skirt

2⅛ yards of red cotton fabric

2¾ yards of cotton fabric (backing)

¾ yard of green print cotton fabric

½ yard of cream print cotton fabric

160 red 8-millimeter faceted beads

16 gold 1-inch-diameter jingle bells

5 yards of ½-inch-wide gold-green-and-red braid trim; fabric glue

For wall hanging

1 yard of cotton fabric (backing)

1 yard of cream print cotton fabric

¾ yard of red cotton fabric

1 yard of green print cotton fabric

240 red 8-millimeter faceted beads

24 gold 1-inch-tall bells with clappers

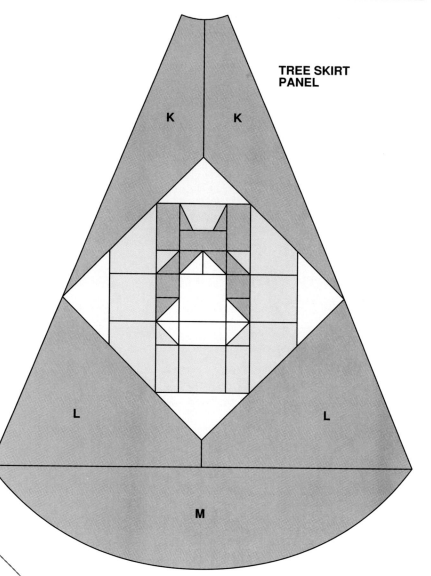

TREE SKIRT PANEL

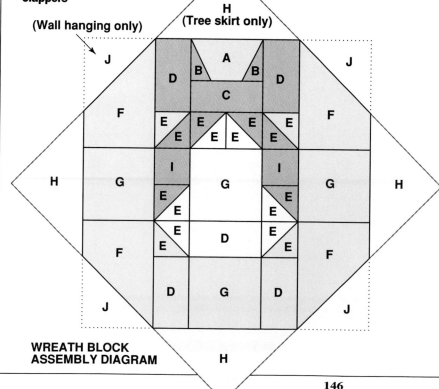

WREATH BLOCK ASSEMBLY DIAGRAM

INSTRUCTIONS

The tree skirt consists of eight blocks, *left,* each incorporated into a panel, *above.* The **wall hanging** consists of 12 blocks, *left,* joined with sashing strips into four rows of three blocks each. All pattern pieces and measurements include ¼-inch seams. Sew seams with right sides of fabric facing. Press seams toward darker fabric. For pattern pieces F, B, K, and L, cut half the pieces, then reverse template to cut remainder.

Trace patterns, *pages 147–150,* onto tracing paper; cut out. Draw around patterns onto cardboard or plastic to make templates; cut out.

For each block, trace around templates onto right side of fabric the number of times specified (the numbers that follow in parentheses are

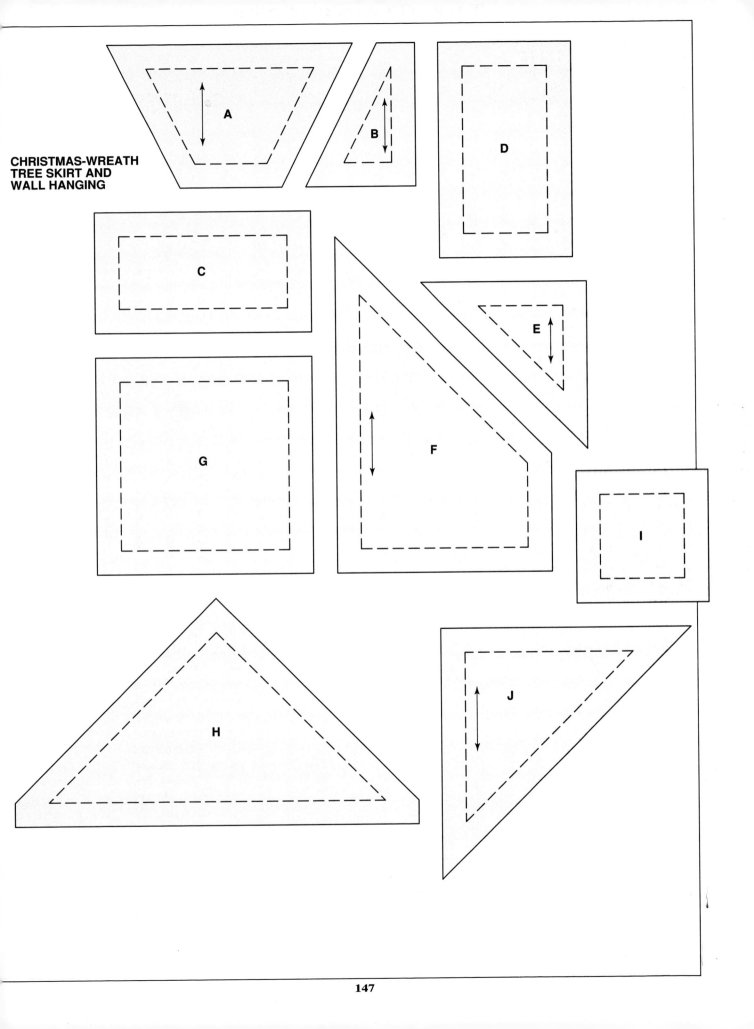

CHRISTMAS-WREATH TREE SKIRT AND WALL HANGING

A

B

C

D

E

F

G

H

I

J

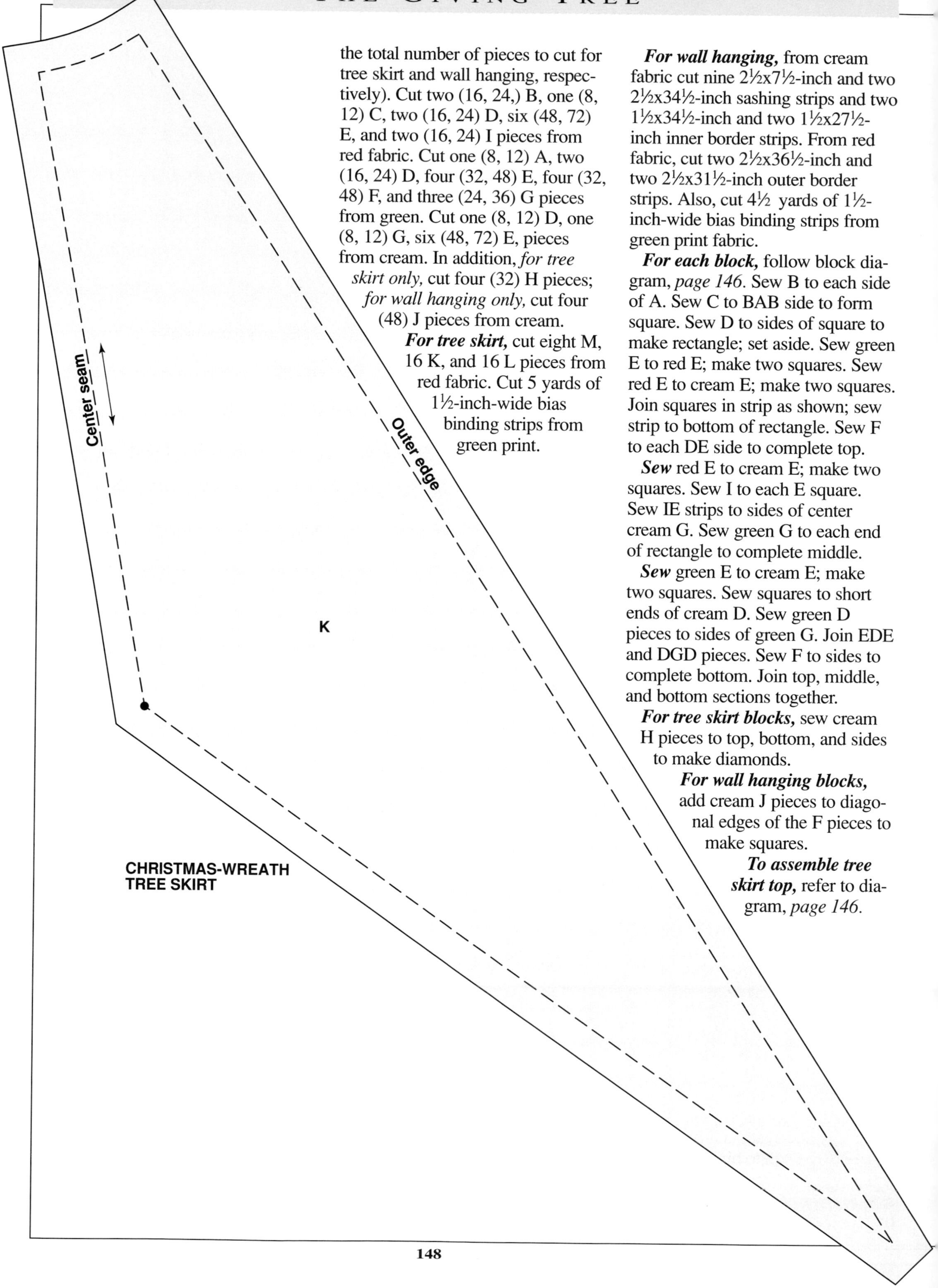

Center seam

Outer edge

K

CHRISTMAS-WREATH TREE SKIRT

the total number of pieces to cut for tree skirt and wall hanging, respectively). Cut two (16, 24,) B, one (8, 12) C, two (16, 24) D, six (48, 72) E, and two (16, 24) I pieces from red fabric. Cut one (8, 12) A, two (16, 24) D, four (32, 48) E, four (32, 48) F, and three (24, 36) G pieces from green. Cut one (8, 12) D, one (8, 12) G, six (48, 72) E, pieces from cream. In addition, *for tree skirt only,* cut four (32) H pieces; *for wall hanging only,* cut four (48) J pieces from cream.

For tree skirt, cut eight M, 16 K, and 16 L pieces from red fabric. Cut 5 yards of 1½-inch-wide bias binding strips from green print.

For wall hanging, from cream fabric cut nine 2½x7½-inch and two 2½x34½-inch sashing strips and two 1½x34½-inch and two 1½x27½-inch inner border strips. From red fabric, cut two 2½x36½-inch and two 2½x31½-inch outer border strips. Also, cut 4½ yards of 1½-inch-wide bias binding strips from green print fabric.

For each block, follow block diagram, *page 146.* Sew B to each side of A. Sew C to BAB side to form square. Sew D to sides of square to make rectangle; set aside. Sew green E to red E; make two squares. Sew red E to cream E; make two squares. Join squares in strip as shown; sew strip to bottom of rectangle. Sew F to each DE side to complete top.

Sew red E to cream E; make two squares. Sew I to each E square. Sew IE strips to sides of center cream G. Sew green G to each end of rectangle to complete middle.

Sew green E to cream E; make two squares. Sew squares to short ends of cream D. Sew green D pieces to sides of green G. Join EDE and DGD pieces. Sew F to sides to complete bottom. Join top, middle, and bottom sections together.

For tree skirt blocks, sew cream H pieces to top, bottom, and sides to make diamonds.

For wall hanging blocks, add cream J pieces to diagonal edges of the F pieces to make squares.

To assemble tree skirt top, refer to diagram, *page 146.*

For each panel, sew K to upper left side of block, stopping at dot. Repeat for the upper right side. Sew K pieces together along the center seam line, beginning at dot. Sew L pieces to remaining sides and sew center seam in same manner. Sew M to bottom. Make eight panels. Join long sides of the panels, leaving one seam unstitched for back opening.

To assemble wall hanging top, first join four blocks in a vertical row, using three 7½-inch-long sashing strips to separate the blocks. Repeat to make three rows. Join the rows using the remaining sashing strips. Sew cream long inner border strips to each side and the short inner border strips to the top and bottom. Add the red outer border strips to sides, top and bottom in same manner.

For tree skirt, cut the backing fabric in half crosswise. Cut each half to measure 26x49½ inches. Sew long sides together, for a 51x49½ inch backing.

To quilt tree skirt and wall hanging, layer the backing, batting, and pieced top. Trim backing and batting, leaving 1 inch extending beyond the pieced top all around. Baste layers together, working from the center outward. Using nylon sewing thread, machine-quilt in the ditch.

Sew binding strips, end to end, to make one long strip. Matching raw edges, sew binding to back, working mitered corners. Press to right side and turn under ¼ inch. Pin mitered corners in place on top; stitch through all layers close to fold. Remove basting stitches.

To finish the tree skirt, sew a bell to points at sides of blocks and the remaining seven bells at scallop indentations around the bottom, referring to photograph. Sew 20 beads to each wreath in a random pattern. Glue trim to binding.

To finish wall hanging, randomly sew 20 beads to each wreath. Sew two bells at base of each bow.

CHRISTMAS-WREATH TREE SKIRT

Top

L

JACK-IN-THE-BOX ORNAMENT

As shown on pages 137, 138–139, and 140, ornament is 3x3x7 inches.

MATERIALS
FABRICS
5x5-inch piece of 18-count white Aida cloth
5x3-inch piece of red felt
Six 3x3-inch pieces of 14-count white perforated plastic

THREADS
#8 braid and cotton embroidery floss in colors listed in key on page 151

SUPPLIES
Needle; embroidery hoop
Erasable fabric marker
Gold seed beads (used as ornaments to decorate the Christmas trees on Jack's box)
Polyester fiberfill; crafts glue
8 inches of ⅛-inch-diameter metallic gold cord
⅜-inch-diameter red pom-pom

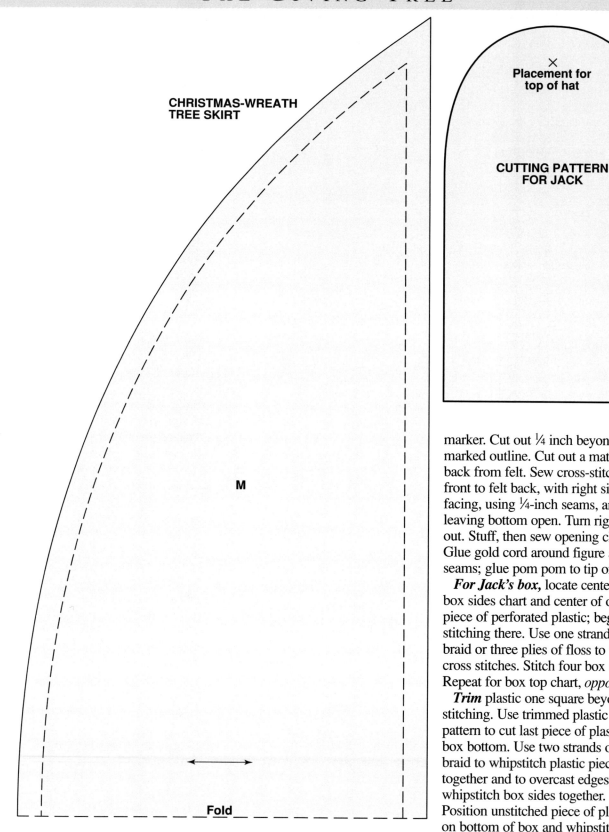

CHRISTMAS-WREATH TREE SKIRT

M

← →

Fold

× **Placement for top of hat**

CUTTING PATTERN FOR JACK

marker. Cut out ¼ inch beyond the marked outline. Cut out a matching back from felt. Sew cross-stitched front to felt back, with right sides facing, using ¼-inch seams, and leaving bottom open. Turn right side out. Stuff, then sew opening closed. Glue gold cord around figure along seams; glue pom pom to tip of cap.

For Jack's box, locate center of box sides chart and center of one piece of perforated plastic; begin stitching there. Use one strand of braid or three plies of floss to work cross stitches. Stitch four box sides. Repeat for box top chart, *opposite.*

Trim plastic one square beyond stitching. Use trimmed plastic as a pattern to cut last piece of plastic for box bottom. Use two strands of red braid to whipstitch plastic pieces together and to overcast edges. First whipstitch box sides together. Position unstitched piece of plastic on bottom of box and whipstitch to box sides. Join box top to one side in the same manner. Overcast top edges of box sides and top.

For hanger, thread needle with an 8-inch piece of red braid; pull braid through the box and knot to form hanger. Slip Jack into box.

INSTRUCTIONS

For Jack figure, zigzag-stitch edges of Aida cloth to prevent fraying. Find center of Jack chart, *opposite,* and center of fabric; begin stitching there. Use two plies of floss to work cross-stitches over one square of the Aida cloth. Work French knots and backstitches using one ply of floss.

Trace pattern, *above right,* onto tracing paper; cut out. Place pattern atop cross-stitched Jack and draw around shape using erasable fabric

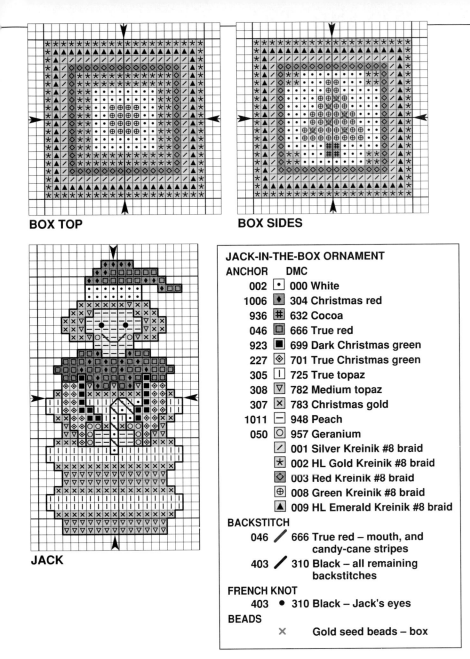

BOX TOP

BOX SIDES

JACK

JACK-IN-THE-BOX ORNAMENT

ANCHOR		DMC	
002	·	000	White
1006	◆	304	Christmas red
936	⊞	632	Cocoa
046	☐	666	True red
923	■	699	Dark Christmas green
227	◈	701	True Christmas green
305	⊡	725	True topaz
308	▽	782	Medium topaz
307	✕	783	Christmas gold
1011	─	948	Peach
050	○	957	Geranium
	╱	001	Silver Kreinik #8 braid
	✶	002	HL Gold Kreinik #8 braid
	◈	003	Red Kreinik #8 braid
	⊕	008	Green Kreinik #8 braid
	▲	009	HL Emerald Kreinik #8 braid

BACKSTITCH

046	╱	666 True red – mouth, and candy-cane stripes
403	╱	310 Black – all remaining backstitches

FRENCH KNOT

403	•	310 Black – Jack's eyes

BEADS

	✕	Gold seed beads – box

ROLY-POLY SANTA

As shown on pages 137, 138–139, and 141, ornament measures 4½x5½ inches.

MATERIALS

Tracing paper; carbon paper
Ballpoint pen
6x7-inch piece of ⅛-inch birch
Scroll saw; drill with ⅛-inch drill bit
Fine grit sandpaper
Acrylic paints: red, peach, black, cream, charcoal gray, medium green, white, and metallic gold
Black permanent ultra fine-tip marking pen
Polyurethane spray

INSTRUCTIONS

Trace pattern, *page 152,* onto tracing paper. Place carbon paper between pattern and wood; transfer body clothing outlines, tracing over lines with ballpoint pen. Cut out Santa with scroll saw. Drill hole in top for hanger. Sand the top surface and edges smooth.

Paint beard and mustache white, fur trim cream, and face peach. Paint hat, coat, pants, and mouth red. Paint boots and belt charcoal, and paint mittens and holly green. Dot eyes and buttons black. Paint holly berries cream. Paint the belt buckle gold. Blush cheeks and nose using a wash of red. Lightly shade

Santa's hair, beard, and clothing using a wash of charcoal gray. Highlight buttons, eyes, nose, and toes of boots with tiny dots or streaks of white. Allow paint to dry. Referring to pattern, *page 152,* draw in all fine details using a marking pen.

To finish, spray ornament with two coats of polyurethane, allowing ornament to dry between coats.

THE CHRISTMAS ROSE

As shown on pages 137, 138–139, and 141, the corsage measures approximately 4x6 inches.

MATERIALS

3 yards of 1½-inch-wide red wire-edge ribbon
1 yard of 1½-inch-wide green wire-edge ribbon
Thread to match ribbons
Sewing needle; polyester fiberfill
3x3-inch piece of buckram
2¾-inch-diameter circle of red felt
Fabric glue; ribbon (for hanging ties)

INSTRUCTIONS

Fold down one end of the red ribbon at a 45° angle with the cut edge extending ½ inch past the wired ribbon edge. Refer to Diagram A, *page 152.* Roll the folded end of the ribbon to form the center of the rose; hand-stitch in place to secure. Fold the ribbon diagonally in the opposite direction; roll two or three times. Refer to Diagram B, *page 152.* Repeat the folding and rolling procedure several times, securing the rolls with stitches as needed to complete the flower center.

Cut ribbon 1 yard beyond the flower center. Pull the bottom ribbon wire, gathering the ribbon. Hand-sew the flower center to the center of the buckram. Spiral the gathered ribbon around the flower center; stitch gathered edge to buckram. Hand-gather the end of the ribbon, tuck the end under, and secure with stitches. Trim buckram ⅛ inch beyond stitching.

ROLY-POLY SANTA

folded ribbon edges slightly as shown in the diagram. To complete the leaf, open up the ribbon. Make two leaves.

Stitch the rosebud wires to the back of the flower so the rosebud shows alongside the flower. Sew one end of each leaf to the back of the flower, arranging the leaves as desired. Sew the felt circle to the back. Attach ribbon ties.

EMBROIDERED DOILY ORNAMENT

As shown on pages 137, 138–139, and 141, doily ornament measures 8x8 inches.

MATERIALS
Tracing paper; fine-tip black marker
Erasable fabric marker
Two 8x8-inch-square Battenburg lace-edge doilies
7-millimeter silk embroidery ribbon: red
4-millimeter silk embroidery ribbon: red, green, and yellow
Size 18 chenille needle
White sewing thread
Sewing needle; polyester fiberfill

INSTRUCTIONS
Trace pattern, *opposite,* onto tracing paper using fine-tip marker. Tape pattern to brightly lit window or light box. Position one doily over pattern, right side up; trace design onto doily using erasable fabric marker.

Refer to pattern and the stitch diagrams, *page 153,* to stitch design on front of one doily. Thread and lock a strand of 7-millimeter red ribbon on chenille needle and work Japanese leaf stitch flowers. Add lazy daisy leaves using green ribbon. Work Colonial Knots flower centers using yellow ribbon and Colonial knots along border using green ribbon.

Cut eight 10-inch-long pieces of 4-millimeter red ribbon. Thread two strips through needle without locking the ribbon. Push needle down through doily from front to back at center of one side near edge. Bring

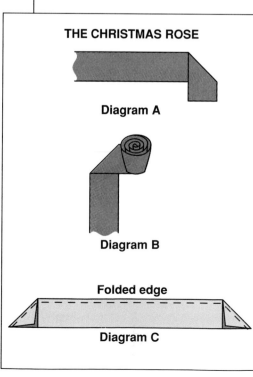

THE CHRISTMAS ROSE

Diagram A

Diagram B

Folded edge

Diagram C

For rosebud, cut a 5-inch-long piece of red ribbon. With right sides facing, sew short ends together using ¼-inch seam allowance. Turn to right side. Hand gather top ¼ inch from the edge using running stitches. Pull threads tight; knot. Wrap the wire, left over from the flower, around a small amount of polyester fiberfill. Poke fiberfill into the bud with wire ends extending from the opening. Gather the open edge using running stitches; pull threads tight and knot. Set the rosebud aside.

For each leaf, cut an 11-inch-long piece of green ribbon. Fold the ribbon in half lengthwise with the wrong sides facing. Fold down both ends of the ribbon at a 45° angle. Refer to Diagram C, *left.* Using running stitches, gather angled and

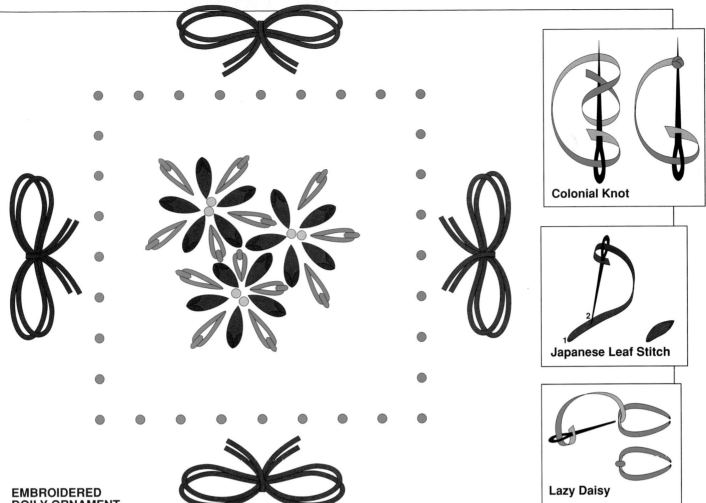

EMBROIDERED DOILY ORNAMENT

Colonial Knot

Japanese Leaf Stitch

Lazy Daisy

needle back up through doily close to first point and remove needle from ribbon. Pull ribbons so tails are same length. Tie ribbon tails into bow. Repeat for each side of doily.

Using a running stitch along inside edge of Battenburg trim, sew unstitched doily to stitched doily, wrong sides facing. Before sewing the fourth side closed, stuff with fiberfill. Sew the opening closed.

TATTED JINGLE FLAKE

As shown on pages 137, 138–139, and 142, ornament measures 6 inches in diameter. Tatting abbreviations are on page 158.

MATERIALS
DMC Cébélia, Size 10 (260-millimeter ball): white
Tatting shuttle; hook for joining picots
Eighteen 8 millimeter jingle bells
White glue; liquid starch

INSTRUCTIONS
Rnd 1: Step 1—Using ball and shuttle, work * ring (r) of [5 double stitches (ds), picot (p)] 4 times, 8 ds, close ring (cl).

Step 2: R of 8 ds, join (j) to last p of previous (prev) r, (5 ds, p) 3 times, 5 ds, cl, reverse work (rw).

Step 3: Chain (ch) of 10 ds, rw.

Step 4: * R of 5 ds, j to last p of prev r, (5 ds, p) 3 times, 8 ds, cl.

Step 5: R of 8 ds, j to last p of prev r, (5 ds, p) 3 times, 5 ds, cl, rw.

Step 6: Ch of 10 ds, rw.

Step 7: Repeat (rep) from * 4 times, joining last r to first r. Tie and cut threads (t&c).

Rnd 2: Step 1—Put 6 bells on thread, then wind thread onto the shuttle, keeping the bells on the ball thread.

Step 2: ** R of 4 ds, (p, 4 ds) 2 times, j to third p of last r on prev rnd, 4 ds, (p, 4 ds) 2 times, cl.

Step 3: R of 4 ds, j to last p of prev r, (4 ds, p) 4 times, 4 ds, cl rw.

Step 4: Ch of 5 ds, (3 p, 5 ds) 2 times, p, 3 ds, rw.

Step 5: R of 4 ds, p, 4 ds, j to fourth p of prev r, 4 ds, j to center p of prev r, 4 ds, (p, 4 ds) 2 times, cl, rw.

Step 6: Ch of 3 ds, j to last p of prev ch, 4 ds, 3 p, 4 ds, slide bell into place, 4 ds, 3 p, 4 ds, p, 3 ds, j to base of prev r, 3 ds, j to prev p, 5 ds, (3 p, 5 ds) 2 times, rw.

Step 7: R of 4 ds, p, 4 ds, j to fourth p of prev r, 4 ds, j to center p of prev r, 4 ds, (p, 4 ds) 2 times, cl.

Step 8: R of 4 ds, j to last p of prev r, 4 ds, p, 4 ds, j to center p of next r on Rnd 1, 4 ds, (p, 4 ds) 2 times, cl, rw.

Step 9: Ch of 14 ds, rw.

Step 10: Rep from ** 5 times. t&c.

Finishing: Trim the ends of the thread and glue in place. Dip the finished ornament into the liquid starch. Let the ornament dry completely. Brush the excess glue away with the toothbrush.

GARLAND TREAT

As shown on pages 138–139, and 142.

MATERIALS

Two lengths of 1-inch-wide white striped sheer ribbon (the desired length for garland) or purchased ribbon tubing from fabric stores
⅛-inch-wide polka-dot grosgrain ribbon: red and green
Wrapped candies

INSTRUCTIONS

To create tubing, hem the ends of both lengths of the striped sheer ribbon. With wrong sides facing, topstitch the lengths together along the long sides as close as possible to the edge of the ribbon.

Cut and tie a piece of grosgrain ribbon around the tubing, about 2 or 3 inches from one end. Slip a wrapped candy inside the tubing, then tie another piece of grosgrain ribbon around the tubing just above the wrapped candy. Continue in this manner, filling the garland.

BOOKMARK ORNAMENTS

As shown on pages 137, 138–139, and 143, bookmarks measure approximately 2⅜x6¼ inches.

MATERIALS

For one bookmark ornament
FABRIC
6-inch length of 2⅜-inch-wide 14-count Aida banding
FLOSS
Cotton embroidery floss in colors listed in key on page 155
SUPPLIES
Needle
2½ inches of ¾-inch-wide flat lace
Fabric glue
1x2-inch piece of paper-backed iron-on adhesive
2-yard strand of embroidery floss

INSTRUCTIONS

Tape or zigzag the edges of the Aida banding. Locate the center of the desired chart, *above* and

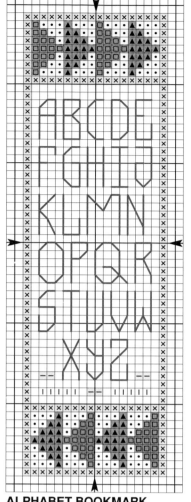

ALPHABET BOOKMARK

PEACE BOOKMARK

opposite, and the center of the Aida banding; begin stitching there. Use three plies of embroidery floss to work cross-stitches. Work backstitches using two plies of embroidery floss.

Glue the trim to the bottom edge of the bookmark, securing cut ends on the back. Following the manufacturer's instructions, iron the adhesive to the wrong side of the bookmark above the design. Remove the paper backing and fold the top corners down to the center at a 45° angle to create a point (see diagram, *opposite);* fuse.

Poke a hole in the top of the bookmark ¼ inch from the point. Cut the 2-yard embroidery floss length in half. Twist strands together. Fold the twisted strand in half; twist again to make a cord. Loop the cord through the hole and knot. Tie ends together; trim.

TASSELED SNOW LACE

As shown on pages 138–139 and 143, snowflakes are 3½ inches wide.

MATERIALS

DMC Cébélia, Size 10 (260-millimeter ball): white
Size 3 steel crochet hook
Liquid starch
Narrow gold cord (hanging loops)
Three 2½-inch-long tassels

INSTRUCTIONS

For frosty-tips snowflake, ch 5, sl st to first ch to close ring.

Rnd 1: Ch 3 (counts as dc), work 17 dc in ring; sl st to top of beg ch-3.

Rnd 2: * Ch 6, sl st in same st, ch 3, sk 2 sts **, sl st in next st; rep from * around, ending last rep at **, sl st to base of beg ch-6.

Rnd 3: Sl st to third ch of ch-6, ch 1, sc in same ch; * ch 6, sc in

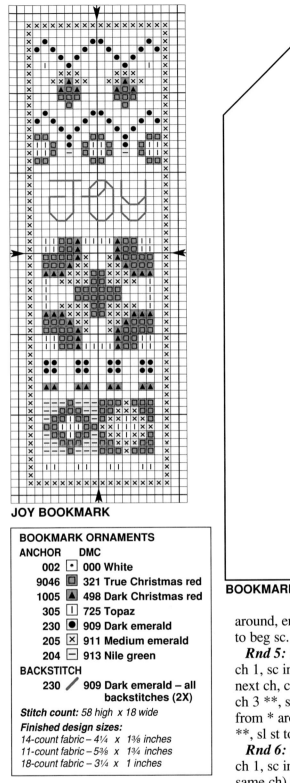

JOY BOOKMARK

BOOKMARK ORNAMENTS PATTERN

next ch, ch 2, sl st in ch-3 sp, ch 2 **, sc in third ch of ch-6; rep from * around, ending last rep at **, sl st to beg sc.

Rnd 4: Sl st to third ch of ch-6, ch 1, sc in same ch; * ch 6, sc in next ch, ch 1, sl st in next ch-2 sp, ch 1, sl st in next ch-2 sp, ch 1 **, sc in third ch of ch-6; rep from * around, ending last rep at **, sl st to beg sc.

around, ending last rep at **, sl st to beg sc.

Rnd 5: Sl st to third ch of ch-6, ch 1, sc in same ch; * ch 6, sc in next ch, ch 3, sl st in next ch-1 sp, ch 3 **, sc in third ch of ch-6; rep from * around, ending last rep at **, sl st to beg sc.

Rnd 6: Sl st in third ch of ch-6, ch 1, sc in same ch; * (ch 6, sl st in same ch) twice, ch 6, sc in next ch, ch 3, sl st in ch-3 sp, ch 1, sl st in next ch-3 sp, ch 3 **, sc in third ch of beg ch-6; rep from * around, ending last rep at **, sl st to beg sc. Fasten off. Make 3.

For six-pointed snow star, ch 5, sl st to first ch to close ring.

Rnd 1: Ch 1, work 12 sc in ring; sl st to first sc.

Rnd 2: Ch 5 (counts as dc and ch 2), dc in same st; * ch 1, sk 1 **, (dc, ch 2, dc) in next st; rep from * around, ending last rep at **, sl st to third ch of beg ch-5.

Rnd 3: Sl st in first sp, ch 5 (counts as dc and ch 2), dc in same sp; * ch 1, sl st in ch-1 sp, ch 1 **, (dc, ch 2, dc) in ch-2 sp; rep from * around, ending last rep at **, sl st to third ch of beg ch-5.

Rnd 4: Sl st in first ch-2 sp; * ch 6, sl st in same sp, (sl st in next ch-1 sp) twice **, sl st in next ch-2 sp; rep from * around, ending last rep at **.

Rnd 5: In ch-6 sp work (sc, ch 3, sc, ch 6, sc, ch 3, sc), draw up a lp in next 2 sl sts, yo, draw through all 3 lps on hook; rep from * around.

Rnd 6: Work 4 sc in ch-3 sp, in ch-6 sp work (4 sc, ch 3, sl st in last sc made, ch 5, sl st in same sc, ch 3, sl st in same sc, 3 sc), 4 sc in ch-3 sp, sl st in sl st; rep from * around. Fasten off. Make 3.

For eight-pointed snow flower, ch 5, sl st to first ch to close ring.

Rnd 1: Ch 1, work 8 sc in ring; sl st to first sc.

Rnd 2: (Ch 9, sl st to next st) 8 times.

Rnd 3: Sl st to fifth ch of ch-9, ch 1, sc in same ch; * ch 4, sc in fifth ch of next ch-9 sp; rep from * around, ch 4, sl st to beg sc.

Rnd 4: Ch 1, sc in same st; * (sc, hdc, dc, tr, dc, hdc, sc) in ch-4 sp **, sc in next st; rep from * around, ending last rep at **, sl st to beg sc.

Rnd 5: Sl st in first st; * sc in sc, hdc in hdc, dc in dc, 2 tr in tr, (ch 6, sl st to last tr made) 3 times, tr in same tr as previous 2 tr, dc in dc, hdc in hdc, sc in sc, sl st in next st; rep from * around. Fasten off. Make 3.

For each ornament, tack 3 shapes together in the center with sewing thread. Dip in liquid starch. Let dry, reshaping ornament during drying process.

Thread cord through the top picot of each snowflake; knot the ends for hanging loop. Tack the loop of the tassel to the center of the ornament.

INDEX

A

Alice-in-Wonderland
  Ornaments 22
Alice-in-Wonderland Playing
  Card Garland 39
Angels
  Angel on Crepe Paper Circle 91
  Sweet Angel Baby 116
  Treetop Angel 117
  Trumpeting Cherub on
    Circle 94
Angel on Crepe Paper Circle 91
Appetizer Medley 12–13
Applesauce-Rhubarb Muffins 59
Appliqué
  Gingerbread Boy Sweater 35
  Peacock Appliqué Vest 9
Apricot Bavarian Crème with
  Raspberry Sauce 106–107

B

Baskets of Goodies 28–29
Beaded, Bejeweled, and
  Bedazzling 145
Beaded Icicles 72
Beaded Star Ornament 89
Blue-Cheese-and-Brandy
  Cheese Log 29
Bookmark Trio 143

C

Candy-Cane-and-Holly
  Place Mat 104
Candy-Cane Cake 105
Candy-Stripes Place Setting 104
Cherry Divinity 87
Chocolate Brownie Mix 58
Chocolate Cashew Clusters 59
Chocolate-Truffle Tarts 24
Christening Dress 10–11
Christmas Bell Bread 106–107
Christmas Dinner Bells 106–107
Christmas Morning
  Buffet 102–103
Christmas Tea Cozy 23
Christmas Tea Party 24–25
Christmas Rose 141
Country Luminaries 73
Crochet
  Antique Bell 106–107
  Inspiration Bell 106–107

Joyful Bell 106–107
  Tasseled Snow Lace 143
Cross-Stitch
  Alice-in-Wonderland
    Ornaments 22
  Bookmark Trio 143
  Elf and Reindeer Party
    Favors 60
  Jack-in-the-Box
    Ornament 140
  Welcome Sampler 10
Crystal-Clear Hobby
  Ornaments 142
Currant-Orange Scones 24

D–F

Diamond Tinsel Ornament 94
Dolls
  Fun Felt Santa Claus 61
  Lovable Elf Santa 121
  Primitive Santa 120
  Red Riding Hood
    Topsy-Turvy Doll 31
  Sweet Angel Baby 116
  Treetop Angel 117
Easy Chocolate-Almond
  Truffles 87
Eggnog 12
Elegant Holiday Wreath 8
Elf and Reindeer Party
  Favors 60
Embroidered Doily
  Ornament 141
Embroidery
  Christmas Tea Cozy 23
  Embroidered Doily
    Ornament 141
Faux Cookie Ornaments 60
Frosty, No-Sew Snow
  Family 118
Fun-Burst Fantasy 145
Fun Felt Santa Claus 61

G–K

Gilded Christmas Corsage 144
Ginger-Berry Lattice Pie 32–33
Gingerbread Boy Sweater 35
Gingerbread Noah's Ark and
  Animals 86
Glimmering Icicles 74
Glittering Goblets 71

Good-Dog Treat 141
Gumdrop Cookie Mix 58
Grandma's Fudge 87
Happy, Lighted Snowman 75
Herbal Snowman 119
Holiday Dress-Up 144
Holly-Stamped Napkin 28
Hot Fudge Sauce 28
Jack-in-the-Box
  Ornament 140
Key Lime Pie 32–33
Kid's Crayon Rain-"Bow" 144
Knitting
  Christening Dress 11
  Soft-as-Kittens Mittens 34

L–O

Lavender Centerpiece 70
Lighting Ideas
  Beaded Icicles 72
  Country Luminaries 73
  Glimmering Icicles 74
  Glittering Goblets 71
  Happy, Lighted Snowman 75
  Lavender Centerpiece 70
  Sparkling Holly Basket 70
  Twinkling Jar 71
Lovable Elf Santa 121
Mini-Bagels with Ham and
  Lemon-Caper Cream 25
Mini-Calzones 13
Mint Divinity 87
Mint-Honey Jelly 29
New Potato Skins 12
Orange-Spinach Toss 102–103
Ornaments
  Angel on Crepe Paper
    Circle 91
  Alice in Wonderland 22
  Beaded Star 89
  Bookmark Trio 143
  Christmas Rose 141
  Crocheted Antique Bell 106–107
  Crocheted Inspiration
    Bell 106–107
  Crocheted Joyful Bell 106–107
  Crystal-Clear Hobby 142
  Diamond Tinsel 94
  Embroidered Doily 141
  Faux Cookie 60
  Good-Dog Treat 141
  Jack in the Box 140

Ribbon Bow 143
Roly-Poly Santa 141
Sugar-Sweet Garland Treat 142
Tasseled Snow Lace 143
Tatted Jingle Flake 142
Tinsel Heart 92
Tree of Christmas Past 82–84
Trumpeting Cherub on Circle 94
Scallop Oval with Sunburst 89
Victorian Star Tree Topper 93
Oyster Stew with
Vegetables 106–107

P–Q

Package Trims
Beaded, Bejeweled, and
Bedazzling 145
Fun-Burst Fantasy 145
Gilded Christmas Corsage 144
Holiday Dress-Up 144
Kid's Crayon Rain-"Bow" 144
Peacock Appliqué Vest 9
Pear-Raspberry Jam 29
Pecan-Cream Cheese Pie 32
Peppery-Plum Barbecue Sauce 59
Pineapple-Carrot Tea Bread 24
Pineapple Marmalade 28
Polynesian Meatballs 13
Primitive Santa 120
Quilted Christmas-Wreath
Tree Skirt and Wall Hanging 140
Quilting
Teatime Quilt 26
Quilted Christmas-Wreath
Tree Skirt and Wall
Hanging 140

R

Raggedy Snowman 60
Recipes
Applesauce-Rhubarb Muffins 59
Apricot Bavarian Crème with
Raspberry Sauce 106–107
Blue-Cheese-and-Brandy
Cheese Log 29
Candy-Cane Cake 105
Cherry Divinity 87
Chocolate Brownie Mix 58
Chocolate Cashew Clusters 59
Chocolate-Truffle Tarts 24
Christmas Bell Bread 106–107

Currant-Orange Scones 24
Easy Chocolate-Almond
Truffles 87
Eggnog 12
Gingerbread 96
Ginger-Berry Lattice Pie 32–33
Grandma's Fudge 87
Gumdrop Cookie Mix 58
Hot Fudge Sauce 28
Key Lime Pie 32–33
Mini-Bagels with Ham and
Lemon-Caper Cream 25
Mini-Calzones 13
Mint Divinity 87
Mint-Honey Jelly 29
New Potato Skins 12
Orange-Spinach Toss 102–103
Oyster Stew with
Vegetables 106–107
Pear-Raspberry Jam 29
Pecan-Cream Cheese Pie 32
Peppery-Plum Barbecue
Sauce 59
Pineapple-Carrot Tea Bread 24
Pineapple Marmalade 28
Polynesian Meatballs 13
Royal Icing 96
Smoky Cheese Ball 29
Spinach Dip in French Bread 12
Strawberry French
Toast 102–103
Tortilla Roll-Ups with Honey-
Vegetable Vinaigrette 25
Whole Wheat Pretzels 59
Victorian Steamed Pudding 88
Red Riding Hood Cape 30
Red Riding Hood Topsy-Turvy
Doll 31
Ribbon Bow 143
Ribbon Embroidery
Christmas Tea Cozy 23
Embroidered Doily
Ornament 141
Roly-Poly Santa 141
Royal Icing 96

S–V

Santas
Fun Felt Santa Claus 61
Lovable Elf Santa 121
Primitive Santa 120
Roly-Poly Santa 141

Satin Ribbon Stocking 85
Scallop Oval with Sunburst 89
Smoky Cheese Ball 29
Snowman Lapel Pin and Button
Covers 61
Snowman-Stamped Napkin 29
Snowmen
Frosty, No-Sew Snow
Family 118
Happy, Lighted Snowman 75
Herbal Snowman 119
Raggedy Snowman 60
Snowman Lapel Pin and
Button Covers 61
Snowman Stamped Napkin 29
Soft-as-Kittens Mittens 34
Sparkling Holly Basket 70
Spinach Dip in French Bread 12
Star Napkin 28–29
Strawberry French Toast 102–103
Sugar-Sweet Garland Treat 142
Sweet Angel Baby 116
Tasseled Snow Lace 143
Tatted Jingle Flake 142
Teacup Gifts 27
Teatime
Christmas Tea Cozy 23
Christmas Tea Party 24–25
Teacup Gifts 27
Teatime Quilt 26
Teatime Quilt 26
Three Christmas Pies 32–33
Tinsel Heart 92
Tortilla Roll-Ups with
Honey-Vegetable Vinaigrette 25
Tree of Christmas Past 82–84
Treetop Angel 117
Trumpeting Cherub on Circle 94
Twinkling Jar 71
Victorian Steamed Pudding 88
Victorian Star Tree Topper 93

W–Z

Wearables
Christening Dress 10–11
Gingerbread Boy Sweater 35
Peacock Appliqué Vest 9
Red Riding Hood Cape 30
Soft-as-Kittens Mittens 34
Welcome Sampler 10
Whole Wheat Pretzels 59
Yummy Treats 58–59

ABBREVIATIONS

CROCHET

ch	chain
dc	double crochet
lp	loop
pat	pattern
rep	repeat
rnd	round
sc	single crochet
sk	skip
sl st	slip stitch
sp	space
st(s)	stitch; stitches

TATTING

ch	chain
cl	close ring
ds	double stitches
j	join
p	picot
r	ring
rep	repeat
rw	reverse work
prev	previous
t&c	tie and cut

KNITTING

beg	begin(ning)
cont	continue
est	established
k	knit
p	purl
pat	pattern
rem	remaining
rep	repeat
rnds	rounds
rs	right side
sl st	slip stitch
st(s)	stitch; stitches
st st	stockinette stitch
tog	together
yo	yarn over

FLOSS/NEEDLES		
Fabric Count	Tapestry Needle Size	No. of Plies
11	24	3
14	24-26	2
18	26	2
22	26	1

CROSS-STITCH BASICS

GETTING STARTED

Cut the floss into 15- to 18-inch lengths and separate all six plies. Recombine plies as indicated in the project instructions and thread into a blunt-tipped needle. Rely on project instructions to find out where to begin stitching the piece.

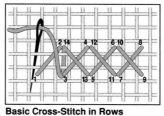

Basic Cross-Stitch in Rows

BASIC CROSS-STITCH

Make one cross-stitch for each symbol on the chart. For horizontal rows, stitch the first diagonal of each stitch in the row. Then, work back across the row, completing each stitch. On linen and even-weave fabrics, stitches are worked over two threads as shown, above. For Aida cloth, each stitch fills one square.

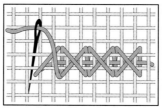

How to Secure Thread at Beginning

HOW TO SECURE THE THREAD

The most common way to secure the beginning tail of a thread is to hold it under the first four or five stitches.

To finish, slip threaded needle under previously stitched threads on wrong side of fabric for four or five stitches, weaving thread back and forth a few time. Clip thread.

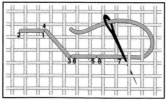

Backstitch

BACKSTITCHES

Backstitches are added to define and outline the shapes in a design. For most projects, backstitches require only one ply of floss. On color key, (2X) indicates two plies of floss, (3X) indicates three plies, etc.

Quarter Cross-Stitch

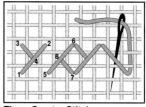

Three-Quarter Stitch

QUARTER AND THREE-QUARTER STITCHES

When a charted square contains one or more symbols positioned in the corner(s), use quarter and/or three-quarter stitches to obtain rounded shapes. On linen and even-weave fabrics, a quarter stitch extends from the corner to the center intersection of threads. On Aida cloth, estimate the center of the square. Three-quarter stitches combine a quarter stitch with a half cross-stitch. Both stitches may slant in any direction.

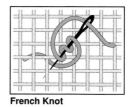

French Knot

FRENCH KNOTS

Bring threaded needle through fabric and wrap floss around needle two full times as shown above. Tighten the twists and insert needle through same place in the fabric. Pull with firm even pressure until floss slides through wrapped thread, making a knot that lies on fabric surface.